NORFOLK
MYST
MURDER

Neil Storey

COUNTRYSIDE BOOKS
NEWBURY, BERKSHIRE

First published 2009
© Neil Storey 2009

All rights reserved. No reproduction
permitted without the prior permission
of the publisher:

COUNTRYSIDE BOOKS
3 Catherine Road
Newbury, Berkshire

To view our complete range of books,
please visit us at
www.countrysidebooks.co.uk

ISBN 978 1 84674 161 6

Cover designed by Peter Davies, Nautilus Design

Produced through MRM Associates Ltd., Reading
Typeset by Mac Style, Beverley, E. Yorkshire
Printed by Cambridge University Press

All material for the manufacture of
this book was sourced from sustainable forests.

Contents

Area Map of Norfolk

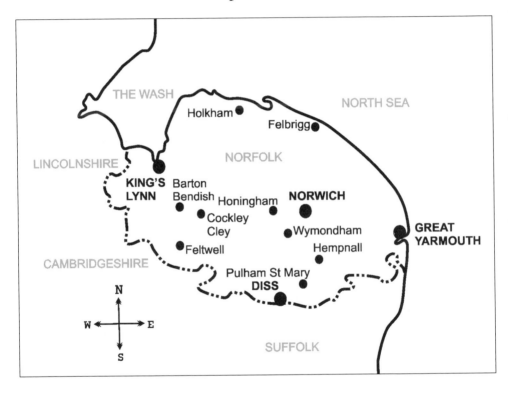

INTRODUCTION

———————❀———————

Over my years researching the history of our beloved county, I have been drawn to some of the more unusual and darker corners of the past. Many of the stories in this volume were once 'big news' but for the most part they have faded from living memory, while others linger on as half-recalled local tales handed down from one generation to another, perhaps given a fleeting mention in a book or faded newspaper that tempts the curious historian to investigate further; others remain ongoing investigations.

The mysterious, the unsolved, the circumstances of murders, extreme violence and executions, particularly those behind closed doors, have proved to be the objects of curiosity and fascination for many. The intrigues and twists cunningly created by the imaginations of novelists can both thrill and chill the reader, as, I hope, will the stories in this volume. The difference is that these stories are true.

From across Norfolk, read of horrific murders such as that of Jemima Stimpson at Wymondham, two horrors in the space of one year at Feltwell, the tragic shooting of Sir Eric Teichman at Honingham and the story of Hubbard Lingley, the last man to be publicly executed Norfolk. Then there are the killers who walked away and remain unknown such as in the case of Lorina Gooderham in Diss, or the headless body found at Cockley Cley; then consider the case of Mary Ann Carrier and ask the question, 'Did she fall or was she pushed?' Open the dark underbelly of Victorian Britain and shudder at the thought of baby farmers at work in Great Yarmouth; wonder if the child buried in Norwich really is the daughter of Mr and Mrs Tom Thumb; or ponder the strange case of William Frederick Windham – was he really mad? Or even Richard Nockolds – was he a violent rebel leader, a scapegoat or a martyr?

There is also the strange case of the 'scareships' in 1909, where a number of independent sightings of mysterious nocturnal aircraft over the county were reported months before any official record of a flying machine crossing the Channel. Were these some of the first recorded instances of visitations by beings from another world? Were the Germans conducting covert missions or was it just mass panic?

Every case has plenty of food for thought. Consider the evidence and enjoy this excursion through the dark, strange and mysterious past of Norfolk – if you dare.

Neil R. Storey

ACKNOWLEDGEMENTS

———————❖———————

In the preparation of this book it has been proved, yet again, that you meet some of the nicest people while researching the darkest stories. There really are too many to mention all by name but I wish to record particular thanks to: Stewart P. Evans and his good lady Rosie, Norfolk Library and Information Service, Norfolk Museums and Archaeology Service, the National Trust, Felbrigg Hall, the Church of St Margaret, Felbrigg, University of East Anglia Library, John Mason and Peter Pilgram at Norfolk Constabulary Archives, Dr Stephen Cherry, Les Bolland, Clifford Elmer Books, Robert 'Bookman' Wright and Elaine Abel.

I also record my thanks to my wonderful students for their interest and comments, especially those at the Pulham Branch of WEA for their assistance with the Elijah Snelling case. Last but by no means least I thank my family, especially my darling Molly and my son Lawrence for their enduring love, support and interest in my research.

WHO KILLED LORINA GOODERHAM?
DISS (1829)

———————— ❖ ————————

Early on the morning of Thursday 4 May 1829 the peace of Diss was shattered as news reached the town of a woman having been found cruelly murdered opposite Mr Cornell's Mill, not far from the Cherry Tree Inn on Brome Lane, only a short distance away. A young woman passing by at about 6.15 am had spotted the body of a woman lying in the road 'in a most unusual posture'. She was lying on her back, with her head a little reclining, her face and neck covered with blood. Her leghorn bonnet lay crushed and bloody near her head; her cap, a set of curls and her pocket were torn off.

The poor woman who had discovered this terrible sight was filled with dread. She froze to the spot, afraid to approach the body, until a man coming from the opposite direction persuaded her to move closer and the full and lurid horror of the crime was revealed. It was plain that the woman had been violently attacked. Her killer had made no attempt to conceal the body; a number of blows had been delivered to the side of her head and face, several knife wounds had been inflicted near her right ear, one of which had divided the temporal artery. Her neck was gashed and there was a deep cut in her breast. The most appalling wound was one which had injured the intestines in several places where 'a considerable part of her bowels gushed out'. The handkerchief of the deceased and the ribbon from her hat were tied tightly around her neck although when a doctor made a closer examination, no marks of strangulation were found. A broadsheet which described the scene concluded, 'from all appearance, her struggles had been severe, and her death horrible, beyond conception'.

Those who discovered the body soon raised the alarm at houses close by and many folks rushed out to see for themselves. Parish authorities were summoned and the body was removed to the bowling green room at the Cherry Tree Inn pending a post-mortem by the County Coroner. Initial enquiries established the body to be that of Lorina Gooderham, aged 46, a colourful character well known in her native Diss. Born Lorina Bryant she had been married twice, first to a man named Noble, with whom she had three children. She married again and had a little girl with her second husband, a Mr Gooderham, who worked as a private watchman in London but because of 'domestic differences' they had been separated for the last 18 months, he living in London and she living in Diss. He did not let his wife and child go without though. He was in the habit of paying her an allowance of five shillings a week.

A meeting of the gentlemen of Diss was convened shortly before noon at the Assembly Room with 'a worthy and reverend magistrate' in the chair to investigate the murder (no Norfolk Constabulary existed in 1829 and thus there were no police officers in Diss).

Witnesses came forward stating they had seen Lorina on several occasions on the days leading up to her murder walking in the direction of the crime scene 'as if she was expecting to meet someone'. She was last seen to leave her lodgings at 8.45 pm on Wednesday 3 May. This was out of character as her landlady recalled she 'was not in the practice of being absent from her home late in the evening, nor ever before to have been absent all night'. Soon after Lorina was seen by a woman and two children who stated that they saw her walking with a respectably dressed man they did not recognise. A woman living about 230 yards from where the body was found claimed she heard a 'peculiar kind of noise at the moment the church clock was striking 12' which she believed 'must have been the groans of the poor creature'.

Coroner Press came with all due haste and convened an inquest on the night after the corpse was discovered. A jury of 'very respectable inhabitants' of the town sat for several hours but the inquest was adjourned pending further investigations. A reward of £50 was offered by the public authorities for any information leading to the apprehension of the murderer. Mr Gooderham returned from London and the funeral of his estranged wife was conducted at 8 pm on the following Sunday. As many as 1,000 people from the town and surrounding villages attended her burial in the churchyard at Diss.

DISS: PRINTED BY K. E. ABBOTT.

A TRUE AND PARTICULAR ACCOUNT

OF A MOST

Cruel and Bloody Murder,

COMMITTED

AT DISS, IN NORFOLK.

"*And it was so, that all that saw it said, There was no such deed done nor seen—unto this day: consider of it, take advice, and speak your minds.*"—Judges xix. 30.

LORINA GOODERHAM, the subject of this melancholy memoir, was forty-six years of age, and was the wife of James Gooderham, whose age is about thirty, to whom she had been married about six years; her maiden name was Bryant, and was a native of Diss. She was twice married, and had three children by the first husband, and one by the present, a girl, now about five years old. From some domestic difference, they had been separated for the last eighteen months, she residing at Diss, and he in London, where he was employed as a private Watchman, and made her a weekly allowance which was regularly paid. On the morning of Thursday, May the 14th, 1829, a considerable alarm was excited in the town of Diss, a parish remarkable for the strictness of its police, and the peaceable behaviour of the inhabitants, by the report of a Woman being found cruelly Murdered, at a very little distance from the town, in a lane called Brome Lane, adjoining the road leading to Lopham. This lane much resorted to, as it afforded a very pleasant walk, and led round to Shelfanger lane, was a very public one. A young woman passing through this lane about a quarter past six o'clock on the morning in question, saw a woman lying in the road, in a most unusual posture; she was afraid to approach, till a man coming in the opposite direction emboldened her to a nearer view of the object; she then turned back, and soon communicated to several of the nearest neighbours what she had seen; many persons now came to the spot, whose horror may be well conceived, when they beheld the murdered woman dead and cold. She appeared as if first struck with a violent blow on her head, and then, while clenched to the ground, her face, throat, breast, and body were barbarously stabbed in a most brutal manner, supposed to have been inflicted with a knife, or small dirk. No attempt was made by the inhuman wretch to conceal the mangled body, as it appears she was murdered on the very spot where first she fell, and on which she was found, lying near the bank extended on her back, with her head a little reclining, and her face and neck covered with blood. Her leghorn bonnet, crushed and bloody, lay near her head; her cap, a set of curls, and a pocket were torn off, and a silk handkerchief was round her neck.

The alarm being spread through the town, the proper authorities took possession of the body, and the attendance of the county Coroner was immediately required. A meeting of the gentlemen of Diss was held in the forenoon, at the Assembly Room; a worthy and reverend Magistrate was in the chair, and the several persons who had last seen the deceased were in attendance, as well as those who had discovered her lying dead in the morning, with all the medical gentlemen who had previously inspected the body; in examining which it appeared that she had received more injuries than were at first apprehended. So determined had been the assassin in the work of her destruction, that he had attacked her in a manner which indicated such diabolical malice, that it seemed as if had she been possessed of

"As many lives as hairs, their great revenge,
Had stomach for them all."

A severe wound was inflicted near the right ear, which had divided the bloodvessel; there was a deep gash in her neck, and also a deep cut in the breast; but the most frightful wound was one about four inches long, on the right side of the body, injuring the intestines in several places, and through this awful gash a considerable part of her bowels gushed out. The handkerchief and ribbon of her hat were tied round her neck as if for the purpose of strangling her, but no marks of strangulation were visible. Still, from all appearance, her struggles had been severe, and her death horrible, beyond conception. A woman living within 230 yards of the spot heard a peculiar kind of noise at the moment the church clock was striking 12, which she thinks must be the groans of the poor creature.

At the investigation, the few persons who had seen her last, said, that she had been seen walking that way several times in the afternoon, apparently expecting to meet some person. She left the house in which she lodged about a quarter before nine on Wednesday evening, it is believed without any money in her pockets, and was afterwards seen by a woman and two children walking with a man, whom they knew not, rather respectably dressed. The woman, in whose house Gooderham lodged, said she had no suspicion of any person or persons on whom to ground a conjecture of being concerned in a transaction so truly horrible; and that the deceased was not in the practice of being absent from her home late in the evening, nor ever before to have been absent all night.

The body was ordered to be removed to the Bowling-green room, at the Cherry Tree Inn, there to await the inquisition of the Coroner, which took place the same evening, before E. Press, esq. one of the coroner's of the county, and a Jury of very respectable inhabitants of the town: but after sitting for several hours, no new light was thrown on the subject, the inquest was adjourned without coming to any conclusion.

A reward of Fifty Pounds has been offered by public authority for the apprehension of the murderer or murderers, but hitherto without effect. On Sunday evening, the husband of the deceased having arrived from London, the funeral took place at eight o'clock, and the remains of the unfortunate victim of revenge and cruelty were interred on the south bank of the church yard, at Diss. From the general excitement which this transaction occasioned among all ranks of people, a great number of persons attended to witness the last solemnities; and it was computed that more than a thousand persons were assembled on the occasion, many of them from the adjacent villages, all eager to collect information. But this most extraordinary occurrence remains involved in mystery, which time seldom fails sooner or later to bring to light;

"For murder, though it hath no tongue, will speak
With most miraculous organs."

And let the murderer or perpetrators of this horrid deed, whoever they may have been, not deceive themselves in a fancied security, for there is an eye to which the most secret and mysterious transactions are clearly discovered, and who in good time, "discovereth deep things out of darkness, and bringeth to light the shadow of death." For there is no place so secret where the perpetrators can hide themselves from him: and that he will infallibly "bring to light the hidden things of darkness, and make manifest the counsels of the heart."

The Coroner's Inquest was resumed on Wednesday morning, May 20th, at 10 o'clock, when a vast number of witnesses were examined, but after sitting till past 11 that night, without coming to any satisfactory evidence, the Jury again adjourned till next morning.

Catchpenny broadside recounting the murder of Lorina Gooderham, 1829.

The inquest was resumed at 10 am on Wednesday 20 May. More witnesses came forward but little new evidence was offered and the hearing was adjourned again. A London constable had been requested for the investigation who checked that Lorina's husband had been at his usual place of work during the night of the murder and thus he was ruled out as a suspect.

The reward offered for information about Lorina's death did give rise to a number of accusations although they were based mostly upon rumour and hearsay. One man, apprehended on suspicion of 'having some knowledge of the person who committed the dreadful deed', was confined in Eye gaol and questioned but to no avail. The strongest suspicion fell upon a young butcher named William Kerry who was said to have 'been intimate' with Lorina.

In the early 19th century there was little or no notion of crime-scene investigation techniques such as fingerprinting, DNA and fibre analysis that are now widely available to police investigators. Questioning had failed to obtain any confession or hard evidence against Kerry so it was believed that the only way to get some indication of his guilt was to confront him with the body and see how he reacted, perhaps in the hope that the sight of his terrible deed would solicit a confession. A long-held belief lingered in this region that when a murderer was confronted by the body of his victim the murderer's fingers would drip blood!

Preparations were made, a jury was assembled and, by order of the magistrates, the coffin was exhumed and removed to the church. In the presence of Magistrates Revd Messrs Manning and Betts, and other gentlemen, the coffin was opened and Kerry was required to approach the body. He was directed to look at it and touch it. He did so, as the *Suffolk Chronicle* described, 'with the utmost promptitude of manner and firmness of nerve: nothing in his look, speech or behaviour exhibited the least symptom of trepidation or discovered the most remote indication of guilt'.

The body was enclosed again in the coffin and reburied. Nobody was ever brought to trial for the murder of Lorina Gooderham. In the absence of any solid evidence, Kerry was set free but the belief that he was involved in the crime lingered among the people of Diss for a long time after.

THE VITRIOLIC
REVOLUTIONARY
NORWICH (1831)

———————❀———————

The city of Norwich has a long history of riot and rebellion but few realise that there was still an active revolutionary movement in the city into the late 18th and early 19th centuries. Although the majority of the activities of the 'Revolution Club' were confined to heated debates over the tables of coffee houses and drinking dens, some of them did become notorious.

After the execution in 1849 of James Blomfield Rush, the infamous Stanfield Hall murderer, a number of publications connected Rush to the Norwich Revolution Club and one of its leading lights, Richard Nockolds.

Nockolds (also spelt Knockells) was at the forefront of the Norwich weavers' riots in January 1830. City weavers were suffering hard times and were now being threatened with lower pay for their work. After their verbal and written complaints were dismissed in a high-handed manner, many city weavers were provoked into militant protest. On Monday 11 January a large body of weavers assembled outside Wright's factory and intimidated the managers. One, Mr Millett, was saved from the mob by Colonel Harvey who courageously seized a man who had thrown a stone or piece of ice. They fled to the Free School but were followed. The gates of the lane leading to the school were shut and the crowd staged a protest outside, sending showers of missiles over the walls. The mayor was alerted to the dangerous situation and with his sheriffs and officers proceeded to the scene with due haste to read the Riot Act and exhort the people to disperse. Most did depart but two men the mayor had especially addressed refused to go and they were conveyed to the Guildhall by coach under the

supervision of Mr Sheriff Beare and
Captain Grint. The removal of these
men again drew a crowd who tried
to rescue one of them before he was
put in the gaol. The keeper of the
prison and his assistants had to fight
hard to get the man inside, the
crowd almost tearing the clothes
from the gaoler's back in the
process.

As if the situation had not been
inflamed enough, the Relief
Committee of the Norwich Court of
Guardians suggested that looms be
set up in the workhouse. The next
day the weavers heard of this
scheme and came en masse to
protest. About 4,000 people
assembled on the road around the
workhouse on St George's Bridge
Street. As the looms were being

The Britons Arms on Elm Hill, historic meeting place of the Norwich Revolution Club.

moved to the workhouse they were seized by the crowd who smashed
them and hauled them into the river. They then tried to enter the
workhouse. The rioters took to the streets and again the mayor and
sheriffs came on the scene. By the time they got there the Riot Act had
already been read by Alderman Thurtell and soon a detachment from
the 7th Dragoon Guards arrived from the cavalry barracks on
Pockthorpe and clattered up and down the streets clearing protestors
with their sturdy mounts and drawn swords.

In the days following, vandalism and many minor scuffles took
place as protestors were left seething. Richard Nockolds' fury
lingered and turned into a cold-blooded, calculated and vicious
attack. He lay in wait for John Wright, one of the master
manufacturers of Norwich, to pass along St Faith's Lane on his way
home. Leaping forward out of the shadows, Nockolds threw
sulphuric acid into Wright's face. Dreadfully injured and partially
blinded by the vitriol, Mr Wright fired his pistol at his assailant but
Nockolds escaped without being recognised by Wright.

This attack drew a great deal of publicity; it was even the subject
of a letter from Edmund Wodehouse published in *The Times* in which
he demanded 'the city mark their abhorrence of the barbarous and

atrocious attempt made upon Mr Wright'. The city officials did set about finding out who the perpetrator was but despite their best efforts and posters offering £100 to anyone identifying Wright's attacker, Nockolds was not given up. Whoever committed the attack remained, for the time being, a mystery.

In November 1830 the voices of disquiet rose again, this time among farm labourers, many of whom had been made redundant by the new harvesting machinery. Activists like Nockolds mustered labourers into rioting mobs who set about breaking machinery and setting fire to haystacks. The first fire occurred on Mr Hill's farm at Briston and throughout the month outbreaks of disorder occurred across the county. A particularly violent mob destroyed John Girling's farm machinery at Paston, the sawmills of Mr Calver at New Catton, and even the looms at Messrs Willett's factory in St Martin's. City and county magistrates had to act fast to restore order. Military mounted troops could not be everywhere at once so hundreds of special constables were sworn in across Norfolk, and emergency measures such as the use of mounted members of the Norfolk Hunt and mobilization of some 200 Chelsea pensioners in the city saw the mobs dispersed.

In the Norfolk quarter sessions of January 1831 the names of 205 prisoners are recorded, 108 of them indicted directly for taking part in the machine-breaking riots. Several of them were sentenced to transportation, while many others received a variety of custodial sentences and fines. At the Lent Assizes Richard Nockolds and three alleged accomplices appeared, accused of setting fire to stacks, the property of farmer William Blake of Swanton Abbott. They were found not guilty of this crime but charged with the same offence on Richard Ducker's farm where Nockolds had left notes at the scene; his handwriting was matched and even the notebooks showing the indentations of the messages written were presented in court.

In the face of this evidence Nockolds stood little chance of evading the charge and he alone was found guilty and sentenced to death. Nockolds was penitent; he confessed to throwing acid in the face of Mr Wright and pleaded forgiveness for the sake of his wife and young family but he was executed, aged 34, in front of Norwich Castle on 9 April 1831. Mercy was shown to his family who were allowed to take his corpse away and exhibit it at his cottage by the cavalry barracks in Pockthorpe. A small charge was made to view his body and a contemporary report concluded 'a considerable sum of money was in this way raised for his widow'.

'SURELY THERE IS NOTHING IN THE WATER?'
HEMPNALL (1839)

───────── ❁ ─────────

Charles Daines, aged 50, was well known in the rural community of Hempnall as an industrious carpenter, a staunch Methodist and a sturdy family man who lived in a modest cottage in the village with his wife and three children. The truth of the matter, that the man and his liaisons behind closed doors in the village told a very different story, was only exposed at his trial in April 1839.

On 11 March Mrs Hannah Daines, bent double with excruciating stomach pains and vomiting, stumbled to the doorstep of her neighbour, Mary Alexander. Fearing her neighbour was in the grip of some severe illness Mrs Alexander sent word to Charles Daines and helped her friend back home where she also discovered two young children and another neighbour, Elizabeth Mills, sitting in a chair; all were racked with similar symptoms. Soon more concerned neighbours came to the house. When Charles returned home he met Mrs Alexander at the door. He appeared surprised at the situation and asked if Hannah was ill. Mary said she was and that Mr Utting the surgeon had been sent for. Daines enquired what she had been taking and Mary said only tea. He replied, 'Surely there is nothing in the water?'

He reached for the kettle, took it outside, rinsed it and refilled it with fresh water. He then pointed at the sop in a basin and enquired if they had eaten any of that. When this was confirmed, he also took that and threw it away. Daines then went into the pantry and brought out some pink powder in a broken basin. He said he had bought it to kill mice and suggested a mouse had been in this basin and then hopped into the pint pot that was used to fill the kettle and this is what had made the women and his children so ill. Despite the neighbours suggesting it may be better to keep both the sop and the basin of powder until the doctor arrived, he threw them both out. Clearly unnerved by the gathering of concerned neighbours, Daines declared he could get medicine quicker than find a doctor and went to the local store to fetch antimony, wine and castor oil.

Mr Utting, the surgeon at nearby Long Stratton, arrived post haste in his pony and trap. He discovered the children and Mrs Mills in grave conditions. Attending Mrs Daines the doctor soon diagnosed poisoning and took possession of the remnants of sop and tea. Three-year-old Elizabeth Daines died at 4 pm and Mrs Mills died a short while later. Charles Daines was arrested on suspicion of poisoning his family. Dr Firth of Norwich analysed the stomachs of both victims along with the sop and tea and found arsenic present in all of them. The pink powder in the broken basin was found to be *nux vomica* (strychnine).

Daines was first indicted at Norfolk Assizes on 11 April for the murder of his daughter but, after half an hour's deliberation, the jury believed there was reasonable doubt and acquitted him. The following morning Daines was brought back to the bar and charged with the attempted poisoning of his wife. Soon the whole sordid tale emerged.

Charles Daines had been having an affair with a local widow, Ann Lloyd, for the past two years. Daines had told Lloyd that his wife was 'an ailing person' not long for this world and that he wanted Mrs Lloyd to stay single until his wife died. Motive ascertained it was soon proved from the evidence of his 18-year-old son John that it was the habit of Charles Daines to start the fire and fill the kettle in the morning. When Mrs Daines took her tea and gave the children their breakfast of sop she used the hot water from the kettle. After just five minutes of drinking the tea she felt ill, her throat was burning, she vomited and soon the children were suffering the same thing. Fearful for their condition she had called her closest neighbour Elizabeth Mills who came to the house and had a cup of tea while she attended to Hannah and her family. Not long after poor Mrs Mills was suffering too.

The jury were convinced of Daines' guilt and returned a verdict of guilty after deliberating for an hour. Passing the death sentence the judge implored Daines to repent and make his peace with God. Upon his return to his cell Daines made a full confession to the prison

The execution of Charles Daines, in front of Norwich Castle, on Saturday,
27 April 1839.

chaplain and also admitted attempting the poisoning on two former
occasions, once by adding arsenic to fried potatoes and then by
adding a little to pea soup, both with little effect. Charles Daines was
executed on 27 April 1839 on a scaffold erected just behind the
gatehouses at the centre of the bridge over the castle ditches. He drew
a crowd of thousands who vied with the Saturday market and cattle
sale to observe the dread sentence carried out.

It was recorded, 'As the clock struck 12 the procession left the
castle for the scaffold ... Daines appeared to be in great distress as he
ascended the platform, supported by two of the turnkeys and
attended by the Reverend Chaplain reading the burial service. The
cap was immediately pulled over his eyes, he turned his back to the
crowd and the drop fell'. He appeared to die an extremely hard death
suffering 'violent struggles and convulsive throes lasting three
minutes ... He clasped his hands, and raised his arms several times
towards his breast as if in the act of prayer, unquestionably showing
that consciousness had not left him. At length his struggles became
less severe and the awful stillness of death followed'.

Daines had obviously not paid the hangman to swing on his legs to
aid him on his way. As he struggled to the last it was recorded that

many who came to observe the execution piously 'expressed their regret that a man of his religious information should have fallen from grace and they trusted his repentance was as sincere as it appeared. Many discussed the policy and utility of public executions but none lamented the punishment of the individual.'

The body of Charles Daines was suspended for an hour then taken down and carried into the castle. Sent for by his family the following Monday, he was buried in the churchyard of St Michael at Thorn on Ber Street, Norwich.

TWICE IN THE POND, ONCE ON THE GALLOWS

WYMONDHAM (1841)

———————— ❁ ————————

John Self, aged 20, was a labourer who lived in a cottage near Wymondham. About two miles from his home lived 15-year-old Jemima Stimpson. Neither knew each other well let alone had any kind of relationship. On 17 July 1841, however, Jemima and 8-year-old George Duffield were working for a Mr Rush, cutting thistles and minding the cows in a turnip field. Self was at work adjacent to the turnip field and when Duffield left to get his lunch, Self went over to Jemima and they struck up a conversation over their meal. After Duffield came back they all returned to their labours until about 4 pm when Jemima left the field with George Duffield who accompanied her as far as the gate of an adjoining field. He watched her on the path until she reached the gap that led into the barley field known as the Gaire's Close. Duffield then noticed Self arrive at the same spot carrying a spade over his shoulder. He saw Self and Jemima then walk on and disappear from view behind a tall hedge.

By 4.30 pm Self was back at home. He sat down to finish braiding a straw hat for his brother until it was time for him to go to bed at his usual hour. Jemima Stimpson had not yet returned home and there was great concern for her whereabouts. A search was mounted but to no avail.

The following day her father, uncles and some family friends retraced her footsteps as described by Duffield. Near the gap at Gaire's Close a large patch of blood and trampled grass spoke of some recent violent deed. They followed a track that had been forced through the barley to a pond where they found Jemima's body. With some difficulty they managed to pull her from the water. Leaving Job

Stanley with the body the other men went for the police and the surgeon, Mr Robert Tunaley. Jemima's body was carried on a hurdle to Mr Hart's barn, near where the girl had lived. Self was the immediate suspect and police constables were soon at his house. He was out but their search revealed a pair of bloodstained trousers hidden behind his bed and a knife known to belong to Jemima in the pocket of his coat. In an outhouse his waistcoat, a bloody cloth, wet stockings and a spade spattered with blood were discovered. PC George Pont was then sent to arrest Self whom he apprehended at Wicklewood workhouse. When asked if he knew anything about the murder, Self replied 'No'. Asked to account for the blood on his trousers, Self claimed he had been working with Jem Wright who had cut his finger 'with some stubbs', but Wright denied this and Self was brought before the Norwich Assizes on 28 July.

At the trial, Self's brother Ben claimed his brother's trousers had not been concealed but were hung over his bed and that the wet stockings were in fact the property of his father who had worn them while working in a ditch. The bloody cloth was indeed the property of John Self; he used it to carry his lunch, but it had become covered in blood after he used the cloth to staunch the blood from a wound suffered by his little nephew. Indeed, all the witnesses credited Self with an exemplary character and a kind disposition, but after just fifteen minutes the jury returned with their verdict. They believed the evidence against Self was damning and they found him guilty. Mr Justice Williams donned the back cap and delivered the death sentence.

When all hopes of commutation or reprieve were gone, Self wrote a confession in the condemned cell. Self said that during the lunch break in question he had asked Jemima to show him her knife. He took it, put it in his pocket and said he should keep it. He then began to play with her but after a time took hold of her clothes in a manner that she much resented. She threatened to tell her mother. Self took pains to deny that he violated her person at any time but returned to work and brooded over her threat. It was then that he thought of murdering her if she would not retract the threat.

When they left work at 4 pm he met her at the gap and he enquired if she was still going to tell her mother. She replied she was and she would 'mob' him for it wherever she met him. Self said she would be telling nothing but lies and seized her by the throat. More threats came from Stimpson so Self threw her down and struck her with his

John Self dragging Jemima Stimpson to her doom, from a chap book produced shortly after his execution on 14 August 1841.

spade a number of times until he believed he had killed her. He added that she only shrieked once with the first blow. He then took her by the heels and dragged her to the pond and threw her in the shallow end. Returning to the place of the murder he found her hat and apron, in which she had tied up some sticks. He hid these in an adjoining field and then returned for his spade by the pond where, to his great surprise, he saw Stimpson sitting about two yards from the edge of the water, blood running from her wounds. Her eyes appeared to 'fix' upon him but she neither cried nor spoke. He grabbed her heels and dragged her back into the water as she clutched at the grass. Self threw her into another part of the pond and put his spade upon her neck to keep her under the murky water. After a while he pushed her into the middle of the pond and left her with her head and mouth above the surface. He swore the blood on the cloth was exactly as his brother had described it, as were the stockings in the outhouse but the blood on the spade and upon his trousers was indeed that of Jemima Stimpson.

Self was executed in front of a large crowd at Norwich Castle on Saturday 14 August 1841. Calm and resigned to his fate, Self was led onto the gallows where he prayed fervently with the chaplain of the gaol and then, having prepared the cap and noose, executioner William Calcraft withdrew the fatal bolt, the trap fell and 'after a short struggle he ceased to exist'. After hanging for about an hour the body of John Self was taken down and buried within the precincts of the prison.

MURDER ON THE ESTATE
HOLKHAM (1851)

———————— ❂ ————————

The charming village of Burnham Thorpe nestles just inland from the sea as one of the beloved 'Burnham villages' clustered along the north Norfolk coast. Burnham Thorpe is famed internationally as the birthplace of Britain's greatest maritime hero, Admiral Lord Nelson. In the summer of 1851, however, the tranquillity of this picturesque corner of the county, along with the Holkham Hall estate, was shattered by a bloody murder.

On the sunny afternoon of 4 July 1851, a young lad named Savory sought a quick route to visit his uncle Mr Doggett who lived and farmed just outside the main village. Savory decided to cut through the small plantation on the Holkham Hall estate. A short distance from the roadside was a secluded sandpit in the middle of the plantation. As Savory passed through it, he was taken aback by a man who appeared to be lying there asleep. He went on and, as he approached his uncle's farm, the boy saw four men hoeing a field of mangold-wurzel. He reported the suspicious character to them. The men said they had heard a gun shot 'about half past one, quarter to two time' and they suggested the boy go back to make sure the man really was just asleep! The boy did not welcome the men's humour and he refused to go. No doubt putting the shots down to one of the keepers, and thinking the fellow mentioned by their master's nephew was just up to a little rabbiting or was a tramp taking a nap, the men kept on working in the field.

The events of the afternoon took a turn for the worse, though, when a donkey cart went trotting by with no driver at about 5 o'clock. One of the men, Mr Yarham, went to hold up the little cart and recognised it as that belonging to John Ayton, the Earl of Leicester's superintendent of the brick and tile works at Burnham Overy. After tethering the donkey, Yarham decided to investigate further and went looking for the 'sleeping' man in the pit. There he found 33-year-old John Ayton, lying on his side. On closer examination Yarham noticed a small wound, like a bullet hole, at the base of Ayton's skull and a pool of congealed blood on the sand.

The cry of 'Murder!' went up. The motive appeared clear; every penny of the £25 5s 6d Ayton was known to be carrying was missing, as was his watch. The local constable was called, and Dr James Young was summoned from Wells.

After examining the body, Dr Young confirmed the wound was from a pistol shot and recorded 'at this wound there was a perforation into which I could introduce a finger'. At the post-mortem he stated, 'On taking off the skull cap, I found a bullet imbedded in the brain, that it had entered about the occipital bone, taking a direction from the lower part of the back of the head to the crown, struck the skull bone and recoiled into the central lobe of the brain causing instantaneous death'. Dr Young had no doubt that the gun had been fired by a person standing behind the murdered man.

Dr Young was also able to add his own testimony to the emerging jigsaw of events. He had been driving with his three daughters along the road by Holkham that very afternoon, shortly after lunch. The doctor had noticed a man named George Groom who had made himself conspicuous by loitering near the entrance to the pit at the plantation. He had recognised him as a man whose family he had treated in the past. The doctor recalled he had even turned to his eldest daughter and said, 'That is a Wells man', as they drove by. A labourer named Joseph Kemp had passed the site shortly after the doctor and had noticed Groom behaving in a furtive manner; in retrospect, perhaps watching for his victim. Following brief enquiries, a shepherd came forward who had noticed Groom near the plantation running and stooping as if he wished to avoid being seen. After the shots were heard Groom was spotted again, this time running away; he even brushed past the shepherd, keeping his head down.

There was a case to be answered and soon Superintendent Kennedy, one of the best officers in the Norfolk force, assembled his men at Holkham New Inn and despatched them across the area to start their enquiries. Meanwhile George Lumley, one of the sturdy constables of Wells, was sent to arrest Groom at the house where he lodged with his father-in-law. Groom was found having his tea. Lumley told Groom

FULL ACCOUNT OF THE Horrid Murder.

On Friday July 4th. Committed on the Body of J. AYTON, Steward to the Earl of Leicester, Holkham, by Geo. GROOM, Aged 32. Norfolk.

Norfolk has gained, and is likely to retain, an unenviable notoriety for crime of the deepest dye. The news of a cold-blooded murder, perpetrated at midday near the seat of the Earl of Leicester, has spread consternation throughout the north-western division of the country. From inquiries made on the spot we learn that the murdered man named John Ayton, 33 years of age, was employed by the Earl of Leicester as superintendent of extensive brick and tile works at Burnham Overy a distance of about a mile and a half from Holkham-hall. It was the usual custom of Ayton to go every alternate Friday, between 11 and twelve o'clock in the morning with a donkey and a cart to Holkham-hall, in order to receive money with which to pay the workpeople and other charges. On returning from the hall, Ayton had to proceed in a direct line through the park to the brickworks passing a small plantation, which enclosed a sandpit, at a short distance from the road side, and about a quarter of a mile from the park gate The place is quite secluded, and well suited for a deed of blood. Lately a man named George Groom, 32 years of age, residing at Wells, which is about two miles from Holkham-hall, was employed at the brickworks: but being discharged, it is supposed that he entertained a revengeful feeling towards Ayton, though he was still employed as a farm labourer on the Holkham estate Groom was well aware of Ayton's custom of going to the hall to receive money, and also of the direct ion in which he returned. We learn, that on Friday last Ayton went as usual to the hall, arriving there between 12 and 1 o'clock, he received from Mr. Shellabear, the chief clerk to Mr. Keary, steward to the Earl of Leicester, the sum of £25 5s. 6d. consisting of sovereigns, half sovereigns, some silver and a £1 note of the bank of Messrs. Gurney. After receiving the money he proceeded along his usual route towards the brickworks, but did not arrive, as expected, to pay the men, after the time he should have arrived, a lad named Savory who was on a visit to his friends in the neighbourhood, and who had occasion to pass through the sandpit before mentioned to the farm of Mr.

Doggett, his uncle, saw as he supposed, a man a-sleep in the pit, and he incidentally mentioned this to four men in his uncle's service who were working in an adjoining field. These men then remembered that between half-past 1 and a quarter to 2 o'clock, they heard the report of firearms, and that they made some remarks to each other on the subject, but they thought nothing more of it. They requested the lad to go back in order to as-certain whether the man he had seen was really asleep or not, but the lad refused to do so not imagining he had seen a dead body At 5 o'clock in the evening one of the labourers saw Ayton's donkey and cart on the road leading from the plantation, and nobody driving. Think-ing this very singular, and remembering what the lad had said, he went into the sandpit, and there saw Ayton lying on his side quite dead, and a small clot of blood on the sand There was a wound on the lower part of the back of the head Dr. Young, of Wells who afterwards examin ed the body, found that at this wound there was a perfor-ation into which he could introduce his finger at the back part of the head. Dr. Young, of Wells who was driving in his carriage with his three daughters, a labouring man named Josep Kemp, and a shepherd saw him at different places not far from the spot where the body was found. In fact, he appears to have been watching for the victim About 1 o'clock Dr Young was passing the sandpit in his carriage, and he distinctly saw Groom who made an obei-sance to him loitering at the entrance of the pit. Dr. Young remarked to his eldest daughter, " That is Wells man," having knowing him for some time and attended to his family. The shepherd had seen him running near the plantation, and stooping, as if he wished to avoid being seen. After the time when the shots were heard the shepherd saw him again near the sandpit, and he brushed past the shepherd, with his head hanging down, George Lamley a constable of Wells went to Groom's house found him there at his tea and took him into custody without saying anything to him till he reached the constable's house. On being searched a £1. note of the bank of Messrs Gurney was found in his possession. When the prisoner was asked how the note came into his possession he said that he had found it about a fortnight before. A watch which belonged to the murdered man also was found on Groom's person. Thus a variety of circumstances tended to prove that Groom was the murderer. On the same evening he was taken before the Rev, R Collyer, examin ed, and remanded to Walsingham prison. Dr. Young evidence was given afterward he was fully committed for trial at the ensuing assizes.

W. Broadhurst Printer Norwich.

Broadside recounting the 'Horrid Murder' of Holkham Steward John Ayton by George Groom on 4 July 1851.

of the charge against him but Groom swore he knew nothing about the murder. On being searched, the police found a £5 note from Messrs Gurney Bank, which Groom said he had found, and a watch containing watch papers with Ayton's name written on them. When the police searched the house they discovered a large pistol that appeared to have been recently discharged. In the bedroom upstairs, tucked under the bed, they also found 15 sovereigns and 12 half sovereigns, the latter wrapped in a piece of paper on which was a note in Ayton's writing.

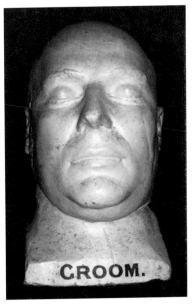

The death mask of George Groom taken during the afternoon after he had been executed in front of Norwich Castle on 16 August 1851.

On the same evening Groom was taken before the local magistrate, the Revd R. Collyer, who remanded him to Walsingham prison. On the following Saturday, Mr H.E. Blyth, the Revd Mr Methold and Revd Collyer held a sitting at the prison and heard the evidence of about a dozen witnesses after which Groom was committed for trial at the next assizes.

Indicted on 28 July, the evidence against Groom was truly damning and his motives were clear. It was known to many on the Holkham estate that Ayton was a creature of habit. Every Friday he would travel in his donkey cart between 11 o'clock and noon to Holkham Hall to collect the wages and expenses payments for the brick and tile yard, then drive back through the park via the West Lodge. Groom had worked at the yard for some time but was, at best, 'unsuitable' for the work and was moved to less lucrative work. He blamed Ayton personally for this and let his feelings be known on the estate and especially in the local inns when he had a few drinks in him. Knowing Ayton's routine, he thought he could kill and rob the unfortunate man without detection.

Standing trial at the Norfolk Assizes, Groom was not defended by counsel. He agreed he was around the scene at the time of the murder but denied killing Ayton. He accounted for the money found under his bed by saying he had found it on the road and insisted, 'Nobody has ever seen me kill a man.' The jury were not impressed by Groom's explanations and instantly returned a unanimous verdict of guilty for the murder and theft. The judge, Mr Justice Cresswell, had no option but to don his black cap and pronounce the sentence of death by hanging. Groom, who used a hearing-trumpet during the whole of the trial, as he was quite deaf, was then withdrawn from the dock.

At 12 noon on 16 August 1851, George Groom was executed on the gallows in front of the county gaol at Norwich Castle. A vast crowd of several thousand came to watch. One reporter, who was present, observed of Groom, 'His awful situation had evidently affected him deeply, both physically and mentally and his outward appearance underwent a great change for the worse during the brief period which has elapsed since his conviction.' When all hope of a reprieve or commutation had passed, Groom sat with the chaplain in the condemned cell and made a confession to the murder.

'MAD' WINDHAM
FELBRIGG (1861)

❁

William Frederick Windham was born on 9 August 1840. He inherited the beautiful Felbrigg estate when he was just 21 and faced the prospect of inheriting more at the age of 28. Sadly, young William had suffered a difficult upbringing. His father, William Howe Windham, could be hot-headed and his mother, the former Lady Sophia Hervey, sister of the Marquis of Bristol, was highly strung and unpredictable. She would pet and caress her son one day, then flog him the next.

William grew quick-tempered and unruly. When he was about 4 years old, he was diagnosed by Mr Nichols, chief surgeon of the Norwich Bethel hospital, as having degenerative weakness of mind. Windham was removed from prep school and was later removed from Eton where he had been placed under the care of the Revd H.J. Cheales, 'a man of great experience in the education and management of boys'. Finding it difficult to introduce even the smallest amount of knowledge into Windham's head, Cheales had tried a variety of ways to deal with the boy. First he tried kindness, then reasoning, then punishment. In the end the only method he found to be effective was personal chastisement and 'the influence of terror'.

William's father died when he was fourteen and his uncle, General Windham, and his mother were appointed as his legal guardians but the General was away on military service most of the time and his mother neglected him. In his teenage years Windham was a tearaway, preferring 'low company and low pursuits' rather than mixing with the society he was expected to enjoy. He was described on more than one occasion as looking and behaving 'like a wild animal'. He was also known to screech and howl, devouring enormous quantities of food 'more like a brute than a rational being'. Sometimes he would eat until he was obliged to go out of the room to be sick, or he vomited in the presence of those at the table with him, hence the other boys nicknamed him 'Mad Windham'.

Then there were the incidents where he dressed up as a police officer on London's Haymarket and rounded up women as they came out of wine saloons and then ordered real police officers to take them back to the station. At Norwich he assumed the character of a detective and while at Yarmouth ran after a party of soldiers in the street claiming to be their captain and ordered them to the guardhouse. On another occasion, while at Felbrigg Hall, Windham made off with a horse-drawn mail cart and pretended to be an officer in the service of the Queen, driving furiously into the crowd assembled in front of a travelling menagerie. He ended up in a bare-knuckle fight with a showman who delivered Windham a fine pair of black eyes.

William had a passion for steam trains which he indulged by dressing as a guard. He would stride up and down the platforms of the Great Eastern Railway herding passengers, slamming doors shut, blowing his whistle and shouting that the train would be 'off in a minute'. It was even known for him to climb into the cab with the driver and fireman and ride the night mail train between Norwich and London. He nearly caused a frightful accident at Cambridge station where he suddenly snatched a whistle from the guard and blew it to start the train. Had it not been stopped in time it would have run into another train. And all of this never caused a stir among the authorities; he simply paid them off. Perhaps he was naïve, or rebelling, or was there something more to it? His mother and uncle were concerned about the large debts the boy was incurring and were afraid there would be nothing of the estate left for future generations.

Then there was his marriage to Agnes Willoughby, a woman described as 'not the chastest of chaste; her favours in love affairs were not few; she was known to the police'. Windham, however, was infatuated. It was claimed that they married despite both knowing that Windham was suffering from 'a foul and infectious disorder'. In her favour Agnes was frank and made no secret of the fact that her reasons for marrying him were not for love but for the future security of her family. William arranged for the execution of a deed whereby his uncle was prevented from inheriting anything. This was the final straw for the General. Only a madman would act as William Windham had done. If he could be shown to be of unsound mind when he did these things, then the marriage and the deed preventing his succession would be declared null and void; thus his uncle ordered a formal commission enquiry into the sanity of William Windham.

The enquiry, held before Mr Samuel Warren QC, opened on Monday 16 December 1861 in the Court of Exchequer, Westminster Hall. It was crowded with many members of the public who were enthralled as more revelations about Windham's behaviour were given in evidence over the next six weeks. Some 140 witnesses were called and a petition 'garnished with an array of names of very considerable position in society' weighed against him. Only his mother refused to add her name to the list.

The evidence presented against Windham by his masters, doctors and people with whom he lodged appeared damning but then on the twelfth day the petitioners were asked to step into the box to confirm to the full court the allegations that they had made in private. The box remained empty. Both the Marquis of Bristol and Lord Alfred Hervey, who had so blackened their young relative's name in the Courts of Chancery, shied from submitting their charges to a public cross-examination. General Windham, who had received initial public sympathy, also refused to repeat what he had declared upon oath in four affidavits.

Public opinion soon changed in favour of Windham and it seemed the proceedings should have closed there and then. However, Mr Warren prolonged the hearing for another 22 sittings maintaining that the respondents should, in equity, be heard. So Windham's supporters stepped into the box one by one; servants from Felbrigg, railway porters, and policemen. After hearing their evidence it was difficult not to conclude that Windham was merely 'a gross noisy fellow, and a bit of a buffoon, whose follies had been no worse than those committed daily and nightly in any barracks. His upbringing explained his predilection for low life'. Even his steam-engine-driving escapades did not seem to be so strange after one witness asserted that 'he had heard in Society how no fewer than three young noblemen were thus addicted'.

On the final day of the inquiry, a rigorous examination was conducted of the questions into the allegations made against Windham's sanity over about three or four hours. Windham acquitted himself in a highly creditable manner and the readiness and intelligence with which he answered a multitude of questions upon a great variety of subjects, some of them of a rather difficult and delicate nature, astonished everyone who heard him. The jury then retired for little more than half an hour and returned the verdict; the foreman, in measured tones, stating that 'the said Mr W.F. Windham, at the time of taking this inquisition, was a person of sound mind, so as to be sufficient for the government of himself, his manners, his messuages, his lands, his tenements, his goods and his chattels'. Upon hearing this, the crowd in the court gave a loud and enthusiastic cheer and the news, on reaching the people assembled outside, was cheered again and again.

The report of these proceedings in *The Times* took pains to point out, 'It has been our disagreeable duty, during the course of the inquiry, to publish evidence of a very disgusting character but the public may be assured that our reports have been purity itself compared with the horrible mass of nastiness laid before the jury.'

After the hearing Windham returned to Felbrigg and carried on his eccentricities. He had an express mail carriage built with the Windham arms emblazoned in gold on the door panels. In this he set out every morning on a journey of 36 miles to Norwich and back to fetch his letters. Soon afterwards he bought a large stagecoach. Wearing the cape of a traditional coachman, he drove passengers at

Felbrigg Hall.

breakneck speeds between Cromer and Norwich; his proud boast being that he would never get into Norwich too late for any passenger to catch the 10.45 am train to London. The sight of this fine liveried coach was truly magnificent but it was a vision best viewed from a distance, for safety's sake. Windham even returned to his antics on the railway. In December 1862 an exchange of letters was published in *The Times* complaining about the 'hurried and uncertain mode of action' of a man dressed as a guard on Cambridge station. The correspondent, a traveller on the train, was concerned enough to ask a porter who the man was. He replied in a sort of half whisper, 'It's only young Windham'. In following letters, Windham said it was not him and the railway denied any knowledge of his actions.

Tragically, Agnes had left Windham for the Italian tenor Antonio Giuglini and a divorce suit was brought. Infidelity could not be established and the case was adjourned but before the hearing the couple were reunited and the exasperated judge made Windham pay not only his own costs but those of his wife and even Giuglini. The tragedies did not end there as Windham's debts had eventually caught up with him and he had no option but to sell Felbrigg. He was finally declared bankrupt in 1864.

Windham resorted to employment in a job he loved – coachman. Those who worked with him recalled that at first he made a good whip. He talked in the broadest Norfolk dialect, accepted with a touch of his hat and a 'Good day, sir' a two-crown tip from every passenger, and exchanged banter with the ostlers at the inns. After ten months he grew bored and began to gallop at breakneck speed into inn yards and deliberately took passengers to the wrong destination. He even staged an overturn. Eventually, after coming to blows with the coach proprietor and spending a night in the lock-up, he 'resigned' and lived in a Norwich tavern on an allowance of £1 a week from his uncle.

William Windham died on 2 February 1866. His memorial stone, high on the wall of Felbrigg church, is inscribed as 'erected by his affectionate wife' but his remains in the crypt below tell their own story. In that catacomb are generations of Windhams. Although decaying, they are encased in lead-lined coffins made from fine woods, wrapped in velvet and studded with splendid ornamentation that speak of their wealth in life and in death. William Windham's coffin is of simple wooden construction and occupies the last compartment in the crypt – the last of the Windhams of Felbrigg in every way.

TOM THUMB'S TRAGEDY
NORWICH (1866)

❁

Barnum & Bailey's circus has entered legend as 'the greatest show on earth' where the most fantastic humans and the most exotic animals in the world were to be found under one big top. Although already a showman, Phineas T. Barnum really made his name because of Charles Sherwood Stratton, the son of a carpenter in Bridgeport, Connecticut.

Charles was an embarrassment to his father. It was hardly the boy's fault – he had stopped growing when he was one year old. Aged four when 'discovered', he was 25 inches tall and weighed only 15 pounds. Barnum immediately saw the child's potential and offered a contract to display him at Barnum's New York museum. The showman initially paid $3 a week plus room, board and travel expenses for the boy and his mother.

By the time Charles arrived in New York, Barnum had him billed as the 11-year-old Tom Thumb, a 'freshly arrived prodigy from Europe'. Barnum knew his audience well; few would have accepted such a young boy as a 'true' dwarf, hence the upping of the age. He knew the Americans' fancy for European attractions so the boy was said to have been born in London and his name was taken from the legendary dwarf knight, Tom Thumb, in King Arthur's court.

Barnum polished the boy, training him in courtly manners, helping him memorise witty quips and several dances and recitations. Young 'Tom' was dressed in fancy costumes. In his youth he often played cupid but as he grew older his stage personas included Hercules, a Scottish highlander, and even Napoleon. Tom Thumb was a smash hit. Barnum took him on a tour of the United States and then headed for Europe in 1844. In Britain, Tom was presented to Queen Victoria and later made his first appearance in Norfolk to a packed house at Norwich Theatre Royal on 29 July 1844.

Barnum went to interview a potential show partner for Tom in 1862. She was Mercy Lavinia Bump Warren. Born in 1841 at Middleboro, Massachusetts, she stopped growing at the age of 10 and by the age of 21 stood 32 inches tall and weighed 29 lbs. Lavinia gave her first formal reception at the American Museum on 2 January 1863. Barnum engineered their meeting but they certainly needed no coaxing to fall in love.

Little more than a month later, on 10 February 1863, Tom Thumb and Lavinia Warren married at New York's Grace Episcopal church in a service attended by 2,000 of the great and the good. Described as the 'fairy wedding', it was attended by George Washington Morrison 'Commodore' Nutt who acted as best man, and Lavinia's even smaller sister Minnie as maid of honour. None of them stood more than 2 ft tall. Never one to miss a trick, while admission to the actual wedding was free, Barnum sold tickets to the reception at the Metropolitan Hotel in New York for $75 each. Police were put on crowd-control duties outside as thousands came to catch a glimpse of the wedding group. The 2,000 people who had tickets were greeted by the newlyweds from atop a grand piano. During their honeymoon the Strattons enjoyed a special reception hosted by President Lincoln at the White House.

On 5 December 1863 it was publicised that the couple had been blessed with a daughter, named Minnie, after Lavinia's sister, and they embarked on a new tour with baby and entourage which brought them back to Britain and Norwich. While they were staying at the Norfolk Hotel on St Giles Street tragedy struck when, on 25 September 1866, young Minnie died after a short illness. The following day her funeral at Norwich cemetery was attended by hundreds of people. The route was lined by locals who came to see the tiny coffin, heaped with 'garlands, wreaths and posies' in the glass-sided horse-drawn hearse. The chief mourners were simply recorded as 'Mr and Mrs Stratton'.

Ironically, Lavinia's sister Minnie died giving birth to a baby in 1878. This latest tragedy really took its toll on the Strattons, perhaps the old wounds of the painful loss of their own child were opened again. In 'Mrs Tom Thumb's Autobiography' published in the *New York Tribune Sunday Magazine* in 1906 Lavinia recalled the loss of her sister. 'It proved one of the greatest trials of my life to go again before the public without her, but it was the life work marked out for me, and I resumed it just as others resume their regular duties after an overwhelming grief. Even now, I do not find it easy to speak of it.'

The couple grew depressed and withdrew from social life and Charles put on a lot of weight, possibly due to a glandular condition. It took all of Barnum's persuasion or rather, as Lavinia put it, a 'liberal offer' to get them back on the road in his 'greatest show on earth' in 1881 but, she said, 'although every convenience and luxury that such a life afforded was ours, it was not to our liking, and at the end of the season we withdrew.' The photographs of them in this later period depict a couple marked by the tragedies that had punctuated their lives and had clearly aged them before their time. They did tour again but just as a couple. Tragedy struck again in 1883 when fire broke out in Newhall House, the Milwaukee hotel where the Strattons were staying. At least 76 bodies were pulled from the charred remains over the next few days; some estimated that up to 90 people had died and it remained the most deadly hotel fire in US history for many decades. The Strattons were saved by their manager, Sylvester Bleeker, whose own wife died after jumping from a high window. Charles never fully recovered from this last traumatic event. While Lavinia was off on tour he died suddenly at home from a stroke in 1883 at the age of 45.

Lavinia remarried in 1885 and carried on touring with her new husband Count Primo Magri, also a dwarf, and a troupe of other dwarves, as well as people of taller stature. They travelled the world, performing plays such as *The Rivals* and *Gulliver Among the Lilliputians.* From the time of her remarriage until her death in 1919, Lavinia

Charles and Lavinia Stratton, 'Mr and Mrs Tom Thumb', with baby Minnie c1864.

denied having ever given birth to a child. She claimed the baby they displayed with them was only part of the show and had been borrowed from a home for abandoned children. When the child grew too large it would be taken back and exchanged for a smaller one. In fact, Lavinia was known to claim that Barnum had obtained the babies only for the duration of the tour from children's homes in the country they were touring, a system she explained as 'English babies in England, French babies in France and German babies in Germany'. Could the child who died in Norwich be one of those borrowed babies or is there more to the story?

Examining the original registrar's book and burial register I found the child's age was recorded as two years old. This tallies perfectly with the age of the Strattons' baby. Significantly the informant on her death certificate is named clearly as Mr Charles Stratton who identifies himself as the child's father; there is no mention of adoption. The Strattons and their manager knew the value of their tours in Great Britain. To make a false declaration, if detected, would mean legal action, public embarrassment and could jeopardise future tours – all of which they knew would be bad for business. If the child had been borrowed, surely it would have been far easier to get the manager to sort out the official paperwork discreetly and honestly without troubling the Strattons?

It is plausible that after the tragic death of their child in Norwich, business sense weighed against grief and not wishing to compromise the rest of the tour they obtained their first borrowed baby. Perhaps it was easier for the Strattons to shut away the memories of the child and its sad death and immerse themselves in their work, the baby displayed with them becoming 'just part of the act'. After the death of Charles, Lavinia would not wish to revisit the painful memories of the past if an easy story of borrowed babies could mean that the painful truth would remain buried.

When Charles Stratton died, over 10,000 people attended the funeral in Mountain Grove cemetery in Bridgeport, Connecticut. Barnum purchased a life-sized statue of Tom Thumb and placed it atop a great column with a fine memorial base. Lavinia died on 25 November 1919 at the age of 79 and was buried next to Charles. The child buried in Norwich shares a common grave with two other children. There is no headstone.

THE LAMENTATIONS OF HUBBARD LINGLEY
BARTON BENDISH (1867)

———— ❁ ————

Benjamin Black was a remarkably steady man of quiet and
unobtrusive habits. In his mid-fifties he was employed as a
woodreeve on Sir Hanson Berney's estate at Barton Bendish. Indeed
he had worked on the estate all his life, as had his father before him.
At about 4 am on Friday 17 May 1867, Black was disturbed by a
gunshot he thought to have come from Burton Leys, one of the estate
woods. He got up and proceeded in the direction of the shot.

At about 6 am a group of labourers walked onto the field by
Burton Leys to hoe wheat. One of these men, Robert Wing, noticed
something lying on the ground by the gate at the entrance to the
wood and, unable to discern quite what it was, went over to
investigate. It proved to be the dead body of Benjamin Black. Lying
on his back, with his arms outspread and his legs drawn up, he was
spattered with blood and riddled with shot. The left side of his face
and neck had suffered the main blast and he was peppered from the
top of his forehead to the top of his left breast. The dead man had
been robbed of what little money he had and an attempt had been
made to rip his watch from him, but his pocket had proved too tight,
the chain had broken and the assailant had fled without it. The
police were summoned and Superintendent Watson of Downham
Market and a number of his officers were soon on site. An
investigation of the murder scene revealed marks of some person
having knelt down near the hedge as if on watch; there were
footprints and the leaves of a maple bush were found scorched by
gunpowder about five yards away from where the body was
discovered.

After initial enquiries, suspicion fell upon Benjamin's nephew, Hubbard Lingley, who was employed as under-woodman and had been found working in the wood where his uncle had been shot on that fatal morning. Summoned to the scene he came running. As tears ran down his face at the sight he wrung his hands sorrowfully crying, 'Oh, my uncle, my uncle!' Lingley drew suspicion to himself after he was first to notice his uncle's purse had gone. PC William Balls later enquired of Lingley, 'You have a gun, where is it?' Lingley replied that it was at home but under further questioning he changed the location to his Uncle Henry's house. When this was found to be untrue, Lingley began to prevaricate and was taken into custody. Afterwards, he showed the police where his gun was hidden, in a thicket of blackthorn about 150 yards from where the body was found. The gun showed signs of being recently discharged; a remnant of percussion cap was still evident. The following day his powder flask was discovered in the trunk of a tree close by and it was learned that Lingley had bought some shot a few days before the murder was committed. Some powder was also picked up near a track in the wood; it was wrapped in the same kind of paper as the shot was sold in. Paper with which the gun had been loaded was picked up near the body and also matched this shot paper. There were even footprints found in the region of the body that matched those of Lingley.

Brought before the Norwich Assizes on 8 August, the evidence already weighed heavily against Lingley. Surgeon William Cator, who had conducted the post-mortem examination on Benjamin Black, said he had taken 15 pieces of shot from the body and he produced them in court. He believed them to be No. 2 shot. Henry Scott the shopkeeper of Fincham confirmed he had sold No. 2 shot to Lingley shortly before the murder and even recognised the paper in which it had been wrapped.

But then there was the matter of motive. It had been suggested that Lingley had plotted to rid himself of his uncle so he could take his job and enjoy all the benefits that went with it but the testimonies presented in court did not support this. The problem was that Lingley's working relationship with his uncle had hardly been harmonious, Lingley had abused his position and pushed his family favours too far. Labourer John Spinks testified to an incident two months before the murder when Black had reprimanded Lingley because he had left his work too soon. Lingley had threatened he would 'do for him'. Maria Pealing recalled she had been talking to

LAMENTATION OF H. LINGLEY.

Within a dungeon in Norwich gaol,
One Hubbard Lingley in grief bewails,
His own kind uncle he did kill and slay,
On a Friday morning in the month of May.
    For that cruel murder he's doomed to die
    On Norwich fatal sad gallows high.

He is doomed to suffer as I relate
On the very tree where Rush met his fate
In health, in vigour, in youth and bloom,
The murderer Lingley must meet his doom.

In the morning early at four o'clock
He fired a sad and dreadful shot
Which caused his uncle's fatal death, wound
Where he fell bleeding upon the ?

A kind good uncle as may be seen
To his wicked nephew he had been ;
Reared him up tenderly and used him well,
And in his cottage with him to dwell

But he resolved he his blood would spill
His uncle Benjamin he wished to kill ;
On Friday morn, the seventeenth of May,
The nephew did his kind uncle slay.

Early in the morning, at four o'clock,
To attract his uncle he fired a shot
And by that spot received the fatal wound.
The murderer flew and left him on the ground

Some labouring men who were passers by,
Saw the murdered in his blood to lie ;
Suspicion did on his nephew fall,
And innocent blood did for vengeance call.

Many excuses did Lingley make,
Not having courage to meet his fate ;
He before a jury for the deed was tried,
And condemned to suffer on the gallows high.

Hubbard Lingley thought when his uncle died
His place to him would not he denied ;
So he was determined to kill and slay,
His uncle dear the seventeenth day of May.

He is doomed to die, nothing can him save,
By the side of Rush in a murderer's grave ;
His bones will moulder till the Judgment day,
How could he take his uncle's life away ?

At Norwich castle he was tried and cast
And his last moments approaching fast ;
The hangman anxious does now await
To terminate Hubbard Lingley's fate.

Oh ! all young men a warning take
Think and consider ere it is too late ;
How could he dare lift his murderous hand.
Base, vile, ungrateful, and cruel man.

H. Disley, Printer, 57, High-street, St. Giles.

Broadside recounting the 'Lamentation' of Hubbard Lingley, 1867.

Lingley three weeks before the shooting and he confessed he and his uncle had had 'a master row' and told her how he took up a hatchet and swore to 'cut the —— down'. On the Saturday before the murder he spoke to her again and told her of another row, adding if his uncle did not 'reckon up' for him he would 'finish him off one day, —— him, I hate him'. Mr Justice Byles delivered a very considered and unbiased summing up but it seems the jurors' minds were quite made up and returned a 'guilty' verdict in less than 20 minutes. His Lordship then passed the death sentence.

In the condemned cell Lingley began to make admissions to Revd J.L. Brown and finally wrote his confession. Lingley claimed he had left his house on the morning of the murder at about 3 am and went to Burton Leys Wood where he was joined by two others who had been poaching. They looked for pheasants' eggs, snared a rabbit and drank liberally from a bottle of gin. They then shot a rabbit outside the wood – probably the shot heard by his uncle. The three came down the glade towards the gate where they found Black. Lingley wrote, 'I have no doubt that he could hear us but we did not care for his hearing us. He could not see us until we got close to the gate. When we came up he could see we had got some pheasants' eggs, as one of them was carrying the eggs in a handkerchief by his side. My uncle said, "You master Hubbard, I have suspected you a long while; now, you've just been promised a house and home as long as you live; I will not screen you one bit." One of my companions said, "Shoot the ——. If you don't, I will. Give me the gun." My uncle said, "I should think you will never do that, you bloodthirsty rascals," and began to get himself behind the clap post of the gate. Seeing that, I immediately clapped my gun to my shoulder and shot him down before he could do so. He twirled partly around from the effect of the shot and fell dead on the spot. My companions then rifled through his pockets and took out his money ... They then tried to get his watch out of his pocket, but it stuck at the top, and I advised them to leave it as the watch was well known by many persons ... I am the real murderer; it was my shot, my gun and my hand which pulled the trigger and caused the death – no one else.'

At 7.45 am on Monday 26 August 1867 Lingley took his last refreshment, a cup of tea. An eyewitness account of Lingley's last moments is recorded in *The Times*: 'He was then summoned to a small office where Calcraft [the executioner] was waiting for him; and he continued to pray earnestly all the time he was being pinioned. A procession was formed in the prison yard headed by the Under-Sheriff (Mr J. Foster), bearing a black wand, the chaplain following in his robes and reading part of the service for the dead. The condemned man came next, supported by the Governor (Mr Pinson), then Calcraft and a few of the prison officers brought up the rear. The prisoner took leave of the chaplain and expressed great hope that the Lord would have mercy upon his soul. He also thanked the Governor for his kindness on earth and expressed a hope they might meet in heaven. The last fatal preparations were completed, Lingley dropped through the gallows trap, and after a convulsive struggle the convict ceased to exist. After hanging the prescribed time the body was cut down and buried within the precincts of the prison.' It was estimated that about 12,000 watched the execution of Hubbard Lingley; they most probably did not realise it was to be the last public execution in Norfolk.

Author's Note: The last public execution in England took place on 26 May 1868 when Michael Barrett the perpetrator of the Clerkenwell bombing was hanged at Newgate, London. On 29 May 1868 the Capital Punishment (Amendment) Act was passed bringing an end to public hanging and requiring executions to be carried out behind prison walls. This Act, however, did allow the sheriff of the county in which the execution took place the discretion to admit newspaper reporters and other witnesses, including relatives of the victim, to the execution. The last execution to be carried out in Norfolk was a 'double' at Norwich Prison on 19 July 1951. In two separate crimes Dennis Moore and Alfred Reynolds had been convicted of the murder of their pregnant sweethearts. The execution was conducted under the direction of Britain's 'No.1 executioner', Albert Pierrepoint, with assistant Syd Dernley appointed as 'No.2 executioner' in respect of Moore, with assistants Harry Allen and Robert 'Les' Stewart.

THE BABY FARMER SCARE
GREAT YARMOUTH (1875)

---❖---

British society was, in the latter half of the 19th century, the epitome of upright morality and sturdy values but behind those well-painted and highly-polished doors, debauchery was rife. Out of these times grew a hideous business all too indicative of the times in which it was practised; it became known as baby farming. If one of the servants or daughters of the house was found to be pregnant and not married, there were a number of horrible options to 'deal with the situation' but only one method really appealed to Victorian sensibilities. The method was simple. Scan the national newspapers for adverts such as:

ADOPTION: *A good home, with a mother's love and care, is offered to a respectable person, wishing her child to be entirely adopted. Premium £5 which includes everything. Apply to Mrs —— by letter only.*

After a short exchange of letters, terms would be agreed. The mother no doubt would have been assured that the baby would be given a loving home with a good family. A short train ride to a large conurbation such as London, a meeting, a cash transaction, baby handed over and the problem would be gone – out of sight, out of mind. The trouble was that despite the dangers of childbearing and high rates of mortality, the supply of unwanted children far outweighed the number of people available to adopt them.

As more and more operatives indulged in the foul trade, the hideous business of baby farming began to be exposed. First indications of the scale of the crime appeared in official reports like that of the Registrar General who stated in the 1860s:

In the last five years within the metropolitan district alone, at least 278 infants were murdered; above 60 were found dead in the Thames or the canals and ponds about London and many more than 100, at all events, were found dead under railway arches, on doorsteps, in dustholes, cellars and the like.

The first high profile prosecution of a baby farmer was that of the Brixton baby farmers Margaret Waters and her sister Sarah Ellis in 1870. Sarah was lucky to get off with 18 months with hard labour; Margaret kept an appointment with the executioner.

The trade continued but baby farmers became more cunning by moving around the country to conduct their trade. Following the high-profile Brixton trial, the public became more vigilant and it would not take much for a baby farming scare to erupt in a town or city. It is tragic to say that in places like Great Yarmouth a baby farmer could come by train, dump a baby and then move quite unnoticed to another part of the country. In Yarmouth there are easily accessible, fast-flowing areas of water where a multitude of sins could be carried away by the tide, including the bodies of unwanted babies. Bodies were found now and then dumped around the poorer areas of towns and cities. Often these were discarded under darkness by parents who could not afford to bury their stillborn child; such incidents would only reach the papers on a slow-news day. Attention, however, would be drawn if *several* babies had been found in the space of a few months, the implication being that if these were the ones found, how many had been disposed of successfully?

In September 1875 the *Yarmouth Mercury* reported the discovery of a dead baby on the riverside edge of Yarmouth Bridge. Soon another body was found in a water cistern and at least two other bodies were recalled as being found dumped in the Rows over the previous four months. Despite the scare and ensuing enquiries, no baby farmer (if there ever was one) was brought to justice in Great Yarmouth and, by the time two more babies were discovered *alive* on doorsteps, little was made of their discovery or subsequent delivery to an orphanage in Norwich.

Probably the strangest disposal of a body at Great Yarmouth occurred in 1877 when a five-month-old baby was discovered at Vauxhall station in a small black bag which had been sent from Liverpool Street. The murderer of this child was never traced nor was the gentleman named on the luggage label.

Another 'little one' discovered at Great Yarmouth during the baby farmer scare of the 1870s.

The hideous trade of baby farming continued across the country and was made vividly public by the coverage of the trial of the steely-eyed Mrs Amelia Dyer who operated in London, Reading and Bristol. She was traced to an address left on the brown wrapping paper she used before tying a brick to her 'parcel' and throwing it into the canal. Dyer was executed in a blaze of press coverage and universal revulsion in 1896.

The last notable baby farmer scare hit Yarmouth on 3 June 1898 when the body of a 'well-grown female child' of about four months was picked out of the river. The public were deeply concerned to learn the unfortunate child had also been wrapped in brown paper – just like the 'parcels' of Mrs Dyer and, just as in the Dyer case, there was a clue. A portion of a label found on the paper had 'ADD' and 'ly' printed on it. This was identified as part of a label belonging to Messrs Sadd & Co of Ipswich. When contacted, the firm stated they had not used that particular kind of label for more than eight months. Investigations led to the belief that the mystery may have had some connection with Gorleston. Suspicion fell upon a 'lady-like person' who had taken rooms in the town. She had drawn attention because she had been so strict in keeping herself to herself and, as stated in the *Yarmouth Mercury*, 'her solitary walks provoked that curiosity which is easily aroused in a place like Gorleston'. Her only visitor was a man who claimed to be her husband, a travelling tobacco salesman who arrived to visit her on Saturdays and left on Mondays. His behaviour was curious, he appeared confused, reserved and uncommunicative. He only ever referred to the woman as 'my wife', he was never heard to speak her name. At a time that matched the probable birth of the female child found in the river, the lady had a baby girl during one of her husband's periodic visits. It was noted 'he was not as pleased as would have been expected of him'. He was said to have remarked, 'Drown the little wretch.'

A few weeks after the birth, the mother and infant accompanied by a 'niece' left the apartments to travel to London but missed the London train. Some of the baby's things were left behind at the lodgings. The woman was eventually traced to Ipswich but the whereabouts of the child was not ascertained, nor does it appear that the woman was positively connected to, nor prosecuted for, the death of the baby found at Yarmouth.

The last baby farmers to be brought to justice in Britain were Annie Walters and Amelia Sach, who also have the ignominious honour of being the first women to be hanged at Holloway in the 20th century, an event that took place on 3 February, 1903. With the advent of widely available contraceptives and the expansion of children's homes and charities, baby farmers became an unmourned thing of the past.

A BAD YEAR FOR THE HANGMAN
NORWICH (1885)

———————❀———————

After the conviction of Robert Goodale for the murder of his wife, Bathsheba, on the Walsoken Marshes near Wisbech, the Norfolk Under-Sheriff, Mr J.B.T. Hales, confidently secured the services of James Berry, the country's chief executioner. Berry was a strongly-built, no-nonsense Yorkshireman. Hailing from Bradford, Berry had had a variety of jobs, including that of railway porter, shoe salesman and even a police constable, but had found his métier as a public executioner. An efficient and methodical man in his work, he was equally adept in his business practice and was the first executioner to use pre-printed invoices. These clearly laid out his terms of employment: £10 for carrying out the execution or £5 if the condemned person was reprieved, plus travelling expenses.

Unfortunately, 1885 was not a good year for executioner Berry. On 23 February he had been engaged at Exeter to carry out the execution of John Lee, aged 19, for the murder of his employer, Miss Emma Keyse, at Babbacombe, near Torquay, where he had been in service since he left school. Lee swore his innocence and had a dream the night before the planned execution that he would not hang for the crime. In what has become, arguably, the most folklore-ridden of all British executions, Lee was made ready and placed on the gallows trap, the noose around his neck. The lever was pushed but the trap refused to open. Lee was removed, the trap was tested and it fell open easily. Lee was put on the trap again, the lever was pushed but still it would not open, despite Berry and the warders adding their weight by stamping on the trap doors. Lee was removed from the chamber and the trap was tested again – it worked with no problems. Lee was

James Berry, the Public Executioner, pictured c1885.

brought on for a third time, made ready to meet his maker – but the trap doors failed again. The chaplain appealed to the governor to intercede but it was the medical officer who stepped forward and said to Berry, 'You may experiment as much as you like on a sack of flour, but you shall not experiment on this man any longer.' Lee was granted a reprieve from death but had to serve a life sentence. He was released in December 1907.

Berry recovered his nerve to carry out the next couple of executions but then there was Moses Shrimpton, a 65-year-old poacher who had killed a police officer. Shrimpton's execution was set for 25 May 1885, at Worcester. Berry worked out the drop from the prescribed table but had not considered the weakness of the old man's neck and almost tore Shrimpton's head from his body. There was no real criticism at the inquest and Berry regained his confidence with the next six executions in the chambers of various prisons.

Berry initially used his own ropes, made to his own design from Italian hemp, ¾ inch thick, 13 ft long, with the noose formed by the rope running through a brass ring spliced into one end (not the hangman's knot commonly used in America and so often depicted in films). Keen to standardise and assure quality, modern governments always preferred to issue operatives with their essential equipment, rather than allow them to use their own; this included executioners' ropes (this was also an attempt to stop the sale of lengths of rope as grim relics). Although made to a similar specification to Berry's own ropes, the one he was to use for the execution of Goodale in Norwich had been supplied by the Government. Even so, Berry liked to use 'tried and tested' ropes at executions so he brought along the one he had used the previous week on John Williams at Hereford. Berry arrived at Norwich gaol and took up his quarters on the afternoon of Saturday 28 November, leaving him time to attend divine service and have the rest of the day clear to ensure all the preparations were made for the execution on the following Monday morning.

Goodale's conduct in prison had been exemplary. He was granted the attendance of a Baptist minister, the Revd T.A. Wheeler. His sister and two sons paid him a final visit on Friday 27 November and, on the same evening, Goodale asked to speak with the Prison Governor, Mr A.E. Dent, who immediately went to the condemned cell with the Chief Warder. Goodale stated he wished to unburden his mind and confessed he had struck his wife because she had said she liked other men better than him. He claimed he had 'struck her down with a piece of iron which laid on the ground near him'. He pleaded extreme provocation and further claimed his wife had fallen down the well after he hit her. He claimed he did not push her and that he had used the bloodstained ladder in an attempt to rescue her, not to push her down. Despite the medical evidence and witness statements in court that confirmed the long history of arguments, threats and violence between Goodale and his wife that weighed against Goodale's claims, the Governor forwarded the document to the Home Secretary and communicated these latest developments to Revd Wheeler. As a result, Wheeler and Mr W.H. Dakin, the ex-Sheriff of Norwich travelled to London and had an interview with the Under-Secretary of State. Neither application led to a reprieve for Goodale.

Berry was informed that Goodale was a big man and that he weighed 15 stone and stood at 5 ft 11 in. He was the second largest man Berry had executed. According to the 'table of drops' Goodale would require a drop of 7 ft 8 in. (William Marwood was the executioner who had laid out the 'table' that helped an executioner to work out a suitable length of rope or 'drop' to break the neck.) Berry was not happy with this length.

Berry had met Goodale in his cell but did not reveal who he was. It was plain to see that Goodale was a physical wreck and despite being a big-framed man, his neck was 'not very muscular' so Berry shortened the drop to 5 ft 9 in. The surgeon asked Berry if he thought this was enough of a drop and Berry assured him it would be sufficient. The scaffold had been erected to Home Office specifications and one man had already been successfully executed on it, but the Governor remained nervous about the whole affair. Apparently, he had already tested the drop on the Thursday morning and again on Saturday before Berry arrived, in the presence of the prison engineer.

The officials for the execution, Under-Sheriff J.B.T. Hales, Mr Haynes S. Robinson the gaol surgeon, Governor Dent and an invited number of local pressmen gathered at the prison early on 13 November 1885. At 7.30 am, Berry conducted his final tests on the gallows in the presence of the Under-Sheriff using a 16-stone weight, as per Home Office regulations. All preparations made, all seemed to have been done 'by the book' and with proper consideration to ensure the execution would run smoothly. Having slept soundly over Sunday night, Goodale woke at 5 am and asked for something to eat almost as soon as his cell door was opened. Revd Wheeler attended Goodale through much of his last hours in the condemned cell.

At 7.55 am, the great bell of St Peter Mancroft church began to toll and the officials gathered by the cell to make their dread procession to the prison bathroom where Goodale would be pinioned. Berry recalled that the screams and cries of Goodale echoed around the prison. His fellow inmates shouted and beat on their doors in reply. Berry continued, 'When I went forward to pinion him he was crying like a little child. Approaching him from behind I slipped the strap around his body. He wriggled to prevent me buckling it, and I had to tell him in a firm tone to be a man.' Eventually it was time for the final walk to the gallows. Goodale refused to move and had to be dragged along, screaming and shouting. The gathered officials and, indeed, Berry had been somewhat unnerved by Goodale's display.

As Goodale drew closer to the gallows he broke down, both physically and mentally, and seemed to pass between a state of collapse and terror in which he repeated 'Oh, God, receive my soul' on the short journey to the gallows where it appeared that his legs would no longer hold him. Two warders held him up while Berry put the final pinions around his legs and the white bag over his head. He adjusted the noose around his neck and, with the fateful lever in hand, asked Goodale, 'Do you wish to say anything?' Goodale replied in the negative and before the church bells of Norwich struck the final chime of eight, Berry pulled the lever, the traps fell open and Goodale was shot to eternity. Berry recorded what happened next in his memoirs, 'We were horrified, however, to see the rope jerked upwards and for an instant I thought the noose had slipped from the culprit's head or that the rope had broken.'

As the black flag was hoisted over the entrance to the gaol to let the crowd outside know that the execution had been carried out, the governor, surgeon and Berry looked into the pit below. Berry continues, having feared the noose had slipped, '... it was worse than that for the jerk had severed the head entirely from the body and both had fallen into the bottom of the pit. Of course death was instantaneous so that the poor fellow had not suffered in any way; but it was terrible to think such a revolting thing should have occurred. We were all unnerved and shocked. The Governor, whose efforts to prevent any accident had kept his nerves at full strain, fairly broke down and wept.'

When the onlookers had recovered their composure an inquest was held by the Coroner E.S. Bignold, Esq in the Magistrates' Room at the Castle. The witnesses all spoke favourably of Berry's thoroughness, pointing out in particular that the executioner was sober. Goodale's head had been severed from his body as cleanly as if it had been done with a knife. The jury considered the evidence and their views were clear: 'Robert Goodale came to his death by hanging according to judgement of law, and in answer to the coroner, the jury did not consider anyone was to blame for what had occurred.'

Although Berry was acquitted of any blame, the 'Goodale mess' haunted him for the rest of his career and probably for the rest of his life. Berry executed a total of 131 men and women, in a career that spanned seven years. In 1892 he retired. After a brief lecture tour he found religion and toured evangelical churches as a respectable preacher who declared he 'gave himself to Jesus'.

Charles Mackie, author of the local historian's essential *Norfolk Annals*, was present at Goodale's execution as a reporter on the *Norfolk Chronicle*. He recalled the execution when he looked back on his career many years later. With some pride he declared he had been present at what could quite justifiably be called 'the last judicial beheading in England'.

A THREAT FROM JACK THE RIPPER
GREAT YARMOUTH (1888)

———————❖———————

By November 1888 national and local newspapers were carrying lurid accounts of 'East End Horrors'. From the horrific and apparently motiveless murder of Polly Nichols on Buck's Row, Whitechapel, concerns arose that an insane serial killer could well be walking abroad in the East End of London. The papers certainly leapt on the story when Inspector Frederick Abberline and his team were despatched from Scotland Yard to investigate the crime on the ground. Earlier knife attacks and murders were soon attributed to the Whitechapel Fiend, mostly by the press. He undoubtedly struck again on 8 September, when the horribly mutilated body of Annie Chapman was discovered at the rear of 29 Hanbury Street, Spitalfields. Fear grew apace as the police seemed to draw blank after blank and were not even able to offer a firm description of the phantom-like killer.

Accounts appeared in the press with witnesses' opinions and reactions to the crimes. Then, just as the story was beginning to lose momentum, a letter arrived at the Central News Agency. Purporting to come from the killer, it taunted the police and threatened more killings. It was signed with a sobriquet which came directly from the streets and society familiar with characters like Jolly Jack Tar, Slippery Jack and Spring-heel'd Jack. The letter was signed – Jack the Ripper. This caught the imagination of many, and a steady stream of letters followed, all of them purporting to be from the killer. On the night of 30 September, Jack the Ripper struck again. The body of 'Long Liz' Stride was discovered by Louis Diemshutz in Dutfield's Yard on Berner Street. Only her throat had been cut and it was assumed the killer had been disturbed. Before the night was out, Jack had found his second victim. Catherine Eddowes was discovered in Mitre Square, more vilely mutilated than any previous victim. Another letter was received at the news agency proclaiming the killings of the night of 30 September as a 'double event'.

The most horrific of all the postal pranks was played on Mr George Lusk, chairman of the Whitechapel Vigilance Committee that had been set up by concerned local businessmen to patrol the streets, at least to deter if not capture the killer. Mr Lusk received a small brown box, postmarked 15 October 1888. When he opened it, he found a letter with the return address of 'From Hell' and half a human kidney. Over the autumn and winter of 1888, hundreds of letters were sent to the police, newspapers and public figures in London and around the country. Most of the missives taunted the police, some attempted to implicate people through malice, others simply revelled in the killings. Occasionally, letters did cause panic, especially if they were sent to areas outside the metropolis. Public fear, hyped by sensational press accounts of the Jack-the-Ripper murders caused people even in the most provincial areas to look over their shoulders and tread more warily after dark. The railways had enabled easy and speedy travel over the length and breadth of Britain and, with the public imagination captured by the media, many wondered where Jack the Ripper would strike next.

On 1 November 1888, at a time popularly described as the 'autumn of terror', a letter arrived at Great Yarmouth Borough Police Headquarters. Addressed to 'The Head Constable of Yarmouth, Yarmouth', it bore a London postmark from the previous day – there was no stamp. The return address was given as 14 Dorset Street, Spitalfields, undoubtedly Ripper country. The letter, written in ominous red ink with a quill pen, said, 'Look out for me on Thursday night at either of the two piers, where I intend to rip up two Norwich women before closing time. So distinguish yourself better than the London coppers – Jack the Ripper.'

Chief Constable William Brogden of Yarmouth Borough had every confidence that the letter was a hoax but others on the force were not so sure. Letters published previously in the London papers that reached Yarmouth were similar in nature – roughly written and badly spelt. This letter was reported as causing concern because it was written 'in good style and the spelling correct'. Clearly some on the force believed that if a person could write with such an educated hand their claims should be taken seriously. The contents of the letter were soon leaked out to the general public.

One Regent Street tradesman was so convinced by the tale that he considered it his public duty to make a formal statement to the police that Jack the Ripper had *actually* been seen in Great Yarmouth. During Wednesday evening and Thursday afternoon another fellow took it upon himself to go along the streets of the town ringing a large bell and, in the manner of a town crier, announced his warning to the female population to stay indoors on Thursday night because the Ripper was on the prowl. The *Yarmouth Mercury* later dismissed this as a 'senseless joke'. To reassure the public, a deliberately noticeable police presence was maintained in the town that week. Along the beaches police vigilance was stepped up but the policemen seemed more engaged in controlling the crowds who swarmed along the sea front and beaches on the night of the threatened attack.

The hideous murder of Mary Kelly at Miller's Court on 9 November 1888 took the climate of fear and horror at the murders committed by Jack the Ripper to an unprecedented level. By 17 November 1888 the *Illustrated Police News*, probably the most graphic and widely read of the sensationalist papers of the time, was carrying news of what they claimed was the seventh and most horribly mutilated victim of the Ripper. Most modern Ripperologists attribute only five killings to Jack the Ripper, those of Nichols, Chapman, Stride, Eddowes and Kelly.

A curious account, also published in the *Yarmouth Mercury* of 17 November 1888, demonstrates how some of the more obscure theories relating to Jack the Ripper suspects were promulgated from London to quite provincial newspapers. After running the Mary Kelly story under the heading 'Another Horrible Murder in Whitechapel', an account of a new suspect was related by Matthew Packer, the Berner Street fruiterer, who had sold some grapes to a man in the company of 'Long Liz' Stride shortly before she was found murdered. Packer stated, 'On Tuesday evening two men came to my house and bought twelve shillings' worth of rabbits off me. They then asked me if I could give an exact description of the man to whom I sold the grapes as they were convinced they knew him and where to find him.' In reply to some questions by Packer, one of the men then said, 'Well, I am sorry to say I believe it is my own cousin. He is an Englishman by birth but some time ago he went to America, stayed there a few years and then came back to London about seven or eight months ago.' The man claimed his cousin had returned a changed

Front page of the infamous Illustrated Police News *for Saturday 17 November* *1888.*

man, having become 'thoroughly harem-scarem', used the term 'boss' as a form of address, like in the infamous 'Dear Boss' letter which had been received prior to the murder of Stride and Eddowes and which the police believed to be from their killer, and while they had walked the streets of Whitechapel and encountered 'unfortunates' he had commented, 'How do you think we used to serve them where I come from? Why, we used to cut their throats and rip them up. I could rip one of them up and get her inside out in no time. We Jack the Rippers kill lots of women over there. You will hear of it being done over here soon, for I am going to turn a London Jack the Ripper!'

The man who related the story to Packer had been motivated to do so after reading the news of the latest horrible murder. Packer stated he felt sure the men were speaking the truth 'as they seemed very much concerned and hardly knew what to do in the matter'. So there were more terrors in the local paper and it caused folks to look over their shoulders again on the Yarmouth beach and down the narrow Rows after dark. Happily there were no Ripper attacks in Yarmouth and the letter was a hoax, but anyone whose imagination was caught by the 'autumn of terror' could never be absolutely sure Jack didn't come on his threatened jaunt to the coast in search of another victim.

DEATH OF THE
MOTHER-IN-LAW
PULHAM ST MARY (1890)

❖

On the bright winter's afternoon of 8 January 1890, a young girl named Laura Hardy was walking down Semere Lane in the direction of the station, not far from the Ram public house at Tivetshall. She noticed a good basket left by the side of the road, and looking closer, she saw blood on the lid and the handle. She did not dare touch it. Then nearby, opposite Green Lane, she saw blood on the hard of the road and the grass, and noticed the fence leading to Mr Reeve's field was broken down. Peering over she saw the body of a woman she recognised, from her clothes, as a neighbour – Mrs Maria Brown, aged 62. She was in a terrible state, covered in mud and gore. She was face down in the ditch with her head about eight inches in the water and with her legs pointing up towards the brow.

Laura ran home to tell her mother and the alarm was raised. Mrs Euphemia Hardy knew Mrs Brown and had seen Mrs Brown's son-in-law, the local vermin catcher, Elijah Snelling, in a little field near their garden while she was having lunch. He appeared to be picking up stones and hurling them in a ditch. When her daughter told her the news, Mrs Hardy went out and encountered Elijah on the road saying, 'For God's sake Snelling, your poor mother-in-law is dead in that hollow up yonder'. He sneered his reply, 'I hope she's in Hell by now'. Mrs Hardy implored, 'O, come and help us get her out'. Snelling was having none of it, saying, 'The old bitch is nothing to me, and I shan't trouble myself after her', and he walked away.

Richard Brown, a Tivetshall engine proprietor, happened to be driving his horse and cart from Pulham to Harleston at the time and hearing of the discovery he drove to the scene. George Hilling, a pauper of the Depwade Union workhouse was on his way to visit his daughter in Tivetshall and arrived at the same time as Richard Brown. Together, they managed to get the body out of the water. As they pulled her out, the extent of her injuries was revealed: her head was 'fearfully battered and covered with blood'. Some who knew the unfortunate woman said her face had been beaten beyond recognition. Brown and Hilling laid her body on the bank and covered her with a shawl. Brown then drove off to summon the police at Pulham. Inspector Short was away in Diss on police business so PCs Massingham and Pooley attended the scene. They supervised the removal of the body to the Ram public house, a service provided by Mr Brown with his cart.

After brief enquiries, the police officers learned Elijah Snelling had been in the vicinity at the time of the attack. Henry Shibley, the landlord of the Ram, said Snelling had been drinking at the pub between about 7 am and 12 noon and had been heard shouting shortly after he left. Jonathan Vincent had called in for a pint and had spoken with Snelling who had said that 'his wife was bad enough but his mother-in-law was far worse'. Mrs Hardy came forward with what she knew and Rosetta Muttocks added she had also seen him pass through her orchard, adding there was 'no public footpath. He had no right to be there'. In fact Snelling was a ne'er do well, known to the police for petty thefts of food, wood and suchlike. He had frequently been reprimanded for the violent outbursts he was susceptible to, particularly when he had a drink in him. Only a few years previously, he had attempted to murder his wife by cutting her throat. While in the lock-up for this attack he had also tried to slash his own throat but his attempt had been frustrated. Brought before the magistrates, bandaged and bloodstained he had been sent down for twelve months.

Left in little doubt that Snelling was involved in the attack, the police officers set out in search of him. It was known that he resided at Rushall and they communicated this information to Police Sergeant Gooch who knew of Snelling's history. Gooch, however, was ahead of them. He had been informed of the case while he was in Harleston and was on his way to Rushall where he was soon informed that Snelling was in the blacksmith's shop.

At the inquest PS Gooch recalled the arrest. 'It was about half past three in the afternoon. Before I could speak he said, "I know what you want. I give myself up for murdering my mother-in-law." I cautioned him, I then brought him into custody at Harleston Police Station. I found a knife (an ordinary bone-handled shut knife) upon him. There was blood upon his boots, on his trousers and on his jacket.' The clothes were produced as described: 'They were made of corduroy material and much bespattered. The boots were of heavy agricultural type and caked with mud and gore. Their soles were shod with heavy nails.' Gooch added that Snelling appeared 'dazed and stupid and seemed as though he had been drinking'.

Wary of Snelling's previous attempt on his life while in custody, Gooch put two constables on watch, with strict instructions that Snelling was not to be left alone day or night. The story soon spread and became a sensation across the district. When Snelling was brought before the magistrates at Harleston Corn Hall the room was packed. Brought up with a constable guarding him on both sides, Snelling maintained a stolid demeanour. The clothes he had been arrested in had been removed as evidence; his appearance at court was recorded as wearing 'a sealskin cap and dressed in a mixed tweed suit. He had a black and white scarf around his neck and his feet were encased in a pair of boots. He is of a slim build, a little over 5 ft in height, and fair, with moustache and slight beard. He did not appear to realise the gravity of the brief but terrible charge read out to him ... His face was pale but firm set and his arms hung limp beside him ... He preserved his sullen demeanour the whole time the proceedings lasted and did not utter a word.' It was commented upon in a number of newspaper reports that his intellect was 'weak'.

At the time of the magistrates' hearing, Dr Legge Paulley of Pulham Market had not conducted a post-mortem but he outlined his exterior examination of Mrs Maria Brown: 'The head and face were covered with mud, which I washed off. I then observed that the face was very much swollen, the features being indistinguishable. There was a lacerated jagged wound at the left corner of the mouth through the cheek, and another through the left nostril. The upper and lower jaw were fractured. The left hand was very much bruised.' He was still unsure, however, without a post-mortem, whether she had died from the wounds inflicted upon her or if she had drowned in the stagnant water her face had been driven into. After hearing the evidence, the magistrates committed Snelling to the assizes.

At the coroner's inquest the findings of Dr Paully's post-mortem were given. He had found 'a fracture of the right collar-bone and of the first and second ribs on the right side; also a fracture of the base of the skull and a contused wound of the scalp over the right ear. The vital organs were healthy. The right lung was much damaged by the broken ribs. There was evidence of death from drowning. The injuries were sufficient to cause death'. After a brief summary of the case from the coroner, the jury returned a verdict of 'wilful murder', the foreman adding, 'It's more the work of a demon than a man.'

On 5 March 1890, 38-year-old Elijah Snelling appeared at the Norfolk Assizes before Mr Justice Denman. Robert Borrett, auctioneer and valuer of Pulham Market had been asked to produce a plan of the scene of the murder and the case was described again by the witnesses and police officers using the map for reference. Dr Paully reported his horrific findings and stated he considered it likely her injuries had been caused from kicks delivered by the heavy boots produced in court. In his summing-up Mr Hansell, Snelling's defence attorney, had a thankless task ahead of him but gallantly questioned the culpability of Snelling for his actions committed under the influence of drink or delirium. Justice Denman was not impressed and riled against the number of insanity pleas used by those arguing the case on behalf of murderers and concluded he 'could not see anything in the case suggestive of reducing the crime to manslaughter'. After five minutes' deliberation, the jury returned the verdict: 'guilty of wilful murder'.

Before passing sentence Justice Denman thundered that this judgement and sentence should be a warning against all those who didn't curb 'their brutish and swinish desires for swallowing liquors', adding, 'I could see no real defence in your case from first to last and I am not surprised that the Jury so soon came to a conclusion.' He then passed sentence of death upon Elijah Snelling. It was remarked upon that, again, Snelling failed to betray any emotion but 'stepped out from the dock rather quickly, as if glad the trial was over'.

A date was set for his execution. However, the concerns of a Mr Francis Dix who had employed Snelling's brother Francis for 20 years, were raised when he read of the case. He had held Francis in high esteem but was aware of a history of mental illness in the family. Both Elijah's uncle and aunt were diagnosed as insane and the aunt had been an inmate of a lunatic asylum for over 20 years. Dix raised a petition and appealed to local MPs who, in turn, obtained the signatures of around 20 medical gentlemen of Norwich. The petition was placed in the hands of the Home Secretary and it was reported that two eminent medical men skilled in the study of mental diseases and associated with important lunatic asylums were sent to assess Snelling. Their report caused the Home Secretary to commute Snelling's sentence of death to one of penal servitude.

MURDER IN ANGEL ROW
GREAT YARMOUTH (1898)

———————❖———————

R ow 44 was known as Angel Row because it passed down the side of the Angel Hotel that stood in the Market Place. Number 1 Angel Row was the first house on the right on the Market Place entrance to the Row. In February 1898, this dingy tenement had been occupied for the last twelve months by 26-year-old Thirza Ann Bensley, known to most as Maud. She had originally come to Yarmouth to go into service but, away from the watchful eye of her parents, she took to earning her living by prostitution. She was well known to the police and had been brought before the magistrates on a number of occasions.

Described as once 'prepossessing in appearance', recently her lifestyle had left its mark upon her good looks. About three years previously, Bensley had begun a relationship with 27-year-old Samuel Frederick Steel who had returned to his hometown shortly after his discharge from service as a trooper in the 19th Hussars. He had found employment as a carter on the Midland & Great Northern Railway in Great Yarmouth. They were very fond of each other but Steel did not care for her liaisons with other men. They often argued over them and their quarrels had escalated into violence. He had threatened her and he had left her on a number of occasions but they usually made up and carried on with each other again. During the separations Steel tended to lodge in Row 73 with his wherryman brother-in-law, John Albert Kerrison.

In early February Bensley brought a sailor back to the house, Steel followed and a fierce argument erupted. Neighbour Mrs King heard Bensley say, 'You bastard, you don't keep me!' Violence ensued; glass was smashed and Bensley broke a stick which she had used to hit Steel and she threw him into the yard. Two policemen came to enquire what the disturbance was. Bensley pleaded, 'Don't lock him up, he's my only love, I have known him three years.' Steel went back to his brother-in-law. He did not go near Angel Row again until about two weeks later when, on Sunday 20 February, he was seen at lunchtime in the Angel Tap by Maud's friend Jane Mary 'Jennie' Danks. On the night of Monday 21 February, Danks and Bensley went to the Angel Tap. Bensley spotted Steel and threw her arms round his neck, kissed him and burst out crying. She asked him if he 'was coming in tonight'. Steel declined but Bensley stood him a glass of six ale and he said he would come back the next night. He kissed her, bade her good night and left. Bensley went home, taking a sailor with her.

The next evening Steel had been drinking with the Kerrisons at the Sadler's Arms, a pub kept by Kerrison's father. At 9.45 pm Steel left them and was next seen in Row 44 at 10.30 pm when he knocked on Maud Bensley's door. Maud was at home with her friend Jennie Danks. Maud answered, 'Come in'. Steel enquired, 'You said come in?' She replied, 'Yes, old partner, where have you been to?' Danks got up from the chair she was sitting on as she knew Bensley had bought it especially for Steel but Steel said, 'I don't want to sit in that, come and have a glass,' so they all went to the Angel Tap where Steel stood treat for a glass of stout for Danks and a glass of six ale for Bensley. Having some remaining in his glass Steel did not order one for himself; he drank that and they all left together at 10.55 pm. Entering Bensley's house Steel reeled, fell against the chiffonier and broke a lamp globe. Maud led him to the couch and put his feet up on it. She knelt over him; he put his arms around her and they kissed. Bensley then set about taking Steel's boots off for him and then helped him remove his coat. Maud asked Jane to go and get a pint of six ale in case Steel was thirsty in the morning. Danks went and fetched the ale in a jug. When she returned the two women managed to get Steel upstairs and into bed (Danks had a bad arm so Bensley had to do most of the work). Returning downstairs Danks decanted the beer into a bottle and adding a piece of sugar took it upstairs with a glass. Back downstairs again Bensley was raking out the grate. She bade Danks goodnight and saw her off from her doorstep, watching until Danks had gone out of the top of the Row. Danks heard Bensley shut the door and turn the key in the lock.

Between 6.30 am and 6.45 am the next morning, Hugh Playford was at a coffee stall in the Market Place near the Angel Tap when he heard screams of 'Murder!' coming from Row 44. He ran across the road and looked down the Row: 'There I saw a woman lying on her back clothed only in what appeared to me to be a night dress. I saw a man [whom he later identified as Steel] bend over her and drag her into the house by the arms. He was dressed in pants and vest only.' Other men had also come running to the scene and Playford followed Joseph John Sadler to the scene. Sadler had been acquainted with Steel and Bensley since the previous October. In his statement Sadler said, 'I was at work on Row 44 on the morning in question ... when I got as far as Bensley's. I noticed blood in the middle of the Row and also on the door jamb, on which there were what I took to be the marks of a hand. The lower sash of the window was out. Whilst I was standing outside the door, I heard the groaning of a man which appeared to come from some little distance. I tried the door and found it fastened.'

The report of someone screaming 'Murder!' on Angel Row was received by Sergeant Herring at the police station. PC Cann had been on night reserve and was then going off duty as PC Wells was going on to take his place with the day shift so both constables set off for the Row. As they passed through Regent Street they noted the time as ten minutes to seven. As they approached Bensley's house, they noticed the blood on the ground opposite the bedroom window, Cann tried the door and found it locked but heard slight moaning. He climbed over the palings into the yard and tried the back door; this was also locked. He called out, 'Maud, are you there?' several times but received no answer. He noted the bedroom window was broken, PC Wells obtained a ladder from the Angel Hotel, where some alterations were being carried out, and Cann climbed up. Noticing blood on the sill and the impression of a bloody hand, he bravely entered the bedroom through the window. PC Wells remained outside.

As Cann made his way into the room, he saw the bedclothes had

A typical Yarmouth Row c1900.

been pulled off and were partially tucked under the bed, otherwise the room did not appear disordered. He checked under the bed; there was no one there. He then noticed a trail of blood at the top of the stairs.

Cann picks up the story in his statement, '... looking down the stairs I saw a man lying there. I went downstairs to have a look at him and noticing his throat was cut, I asked, "What's the matter?" He just turned his eyes up but said nothing. He was bleeding. I went upstairs again to take my coat and helmet off because the stairs were so narrow I could not get down. A lamp was burning in the bedroom and I turned it on full and took it downstairs. The man was lying in the angle of the staircase and, as I squeezed past him, he again turned up his eyes but said nothing. On getting from the staircase into the kitchen I saw Bensley lying on the floor, full length, with the exception that one knee was drawn up a little. She had nothing on but a short chemise and her head appeared to be nearly severed from her body. There was no sign of a struggle having taken place and the only blood in the room was a great pool round her head, which had flowed from her throat as she lay ... I went upstairs to call Wells and said, "Maud is dead and the man is lying on the stairs." Wells came in by the window and coming down the stairs, he took hold of the man's head and I got his feet. As soon as we drew him off one stair he sprang to his feet and came for me, I slipped down the stairs and swung him round into the room. Wells being higher up could not render much help. I tried to keep him off by his shoulders. I could not touch his throat as it was cut in the fleshy part. He made grabs at my neck and after scratching the side of my face he caught hold of a black silk handkerchief around my neck. He might have strangled me with this for I could not break his hold till I got out my knife and cut the handkerchief through. [Steel then fastened his teeth into PC Cann's shoulder and lashed out with his legs.] Wells now came to my assistance but he was knocked over, so was the table; the lamp went out, pictures were knocked down but we got him on the ground, where he kicked and struggled. He was like an eel. Then he quietened down and Wells kept him down while I went to the door to summon assistance.' Cann sent a young man named Childs to fetch Dr Lettis. They were also soon joined by PC Platten who Cann sent to the hospital for the ambulance. Sergeant Herring and PC Snelling then arrived and Steel was handcuffed. Dr Lettis bandaged Steel's throat and he was removed to hospital wrapped in a sheet and a counterpane; although the gash appeared serious he was expected to recover.

Conducting a search of the house PC Cann found a bloodstained razor on the floor, by the side of the fireplace. It bore mute testimony to its use as a murder weapon: 'Its brittle keen edge had suffered and it was as jagged as a saw.' Dr Lettis examined the horribly mutilated body of Maud Bensley. Her head was bruised and broken, laid at a sickening angle to her almost naked trunk as it only remained attached to her body by a thin piece of unsevered flesh and bone. His closer examination revealed that blood had spread across the floor and had sprayed up the wall and even on the ceiling. The gashes to her neck 'went into the collar bone and cut clean through all the structures of the neck – the wind pipe, the carotid artery, large blood vessels and nerves and into the vertebral column exposing the spinal column'. Other injuries consisted of a cut on the left side of the body, some eight inches long and an inch deep in some parts. There was a further injury on her back some four or five inches long, her hand and wrists were also badly gashed. Dr Lettis was of the opinion the cuts to her body were caused as she tried to defend herself against Steel's murderous attack. The damage to the sash window led some to believe Steel had pushed her out of it in his fury; others thought she had tried to escape or call for help out of the window. She made for the stairs, perhaps Steel pushed her down, she managed to scramble out of the door where she collapsed and bled on the pavings of the Row. Steel was hard on her heels, he pulled her back in and then cut her throat. The wounds he inflicted upon her would clearly have proved fatal. Steel then picked up an engineer's wrench he had used at the house as a poker and rained frenzied blows upon her head, completely smashing the frontal and occipital bones of her skull and fracturing her lower jaw; two fragments of skull and brain matter were found spattered across the floor of the room. The wrench, measuring 15 inches long, was found between the body and the fireplace covered in blood and gore with some hair still stuck to it. The body was covered up and police officers were placed on guard. They were certainly kept busy as news got around the town and a crowd of sightseers came to Row 44.

The inquest led by Borough Coroner J.T. Waters, Esq was opened in the evening to a packed room on the ground floor of the Angel Hotel. After introductory remarks and a description of how Bensley was discovered, the jurors and the Chief Constable went to view the body, described, without exaggeration, as 'shockingly mutilated'. Mrs Ellen King, Bensley's next-door neighbour, gave evidence. She had heard some words being exchanged then she heard Maud scream and call out, 'Oh, Mrs King, Mrs King'. She opened her window to ask what the matter was. She then heard Steel say, 'You have broken my heart and ruined me and now I'll murder you, you bitch.' Evidence was given by Maud's father, Charles Bensley, who confirmed her identity and related what little he had known of her of late. Then the inquest was adjourned pending a post-mortem and further investigations. When the inquest was reconvened, the jury unanimously returned a verdict of wilful murder against Steel who was formally committed on the coroner's warrant.

On 28 February Steel was brought before the magistrates and charged with the murder of Thirza Ann Bensley. Escorted to the dock by PCs Wells and Chase, the *Yarmouth Mercury* observed of Steel, 'There was nothing about the man to lead one to associate him with such a horrible crime. His appearance and dress were most respectable. He wore no collar owing to the presence of surgical bandages round his throat ... He wore a long overcoat with big lapels, which made him look smart, an effect which was heightened by the smooth way his hair was brushed, parted and curled – after the soldier fashion. He wore a slight moustache, being otherwise clean-shaven. His face was stolid, sullen and expressionless, and except one brief minute (when the name of his paramour was mentioned and an allusion to the razor was made) he gave no outward sign of any particular interest in what was going on.' An eyewitness in the court recalled the moment of Steel's reaction: '... he seemed to be seized with a momentary spasm. He gripped the rail in front of him and his face became convulsed, as if he was trying to keep back the evil within.' The hearing was adjourned and the tragic remains of Thirza Ann Bensley were buried in secret at 8 am on Saturday 5 March 1898. There were no wreaths upon her polished wood coffin; her sole mourners were her stepmother and three stepsisters. The Chief Constable, Inspector Hardesty and four constables accompanied the sad procession which passed via Northgate Street to the cemetery where the four police officers bore the coffin to the grave which occupies a position in the north-east corner of the ground, almost next to the wall. In the presence of the small company gathered, Mr Walter Flaxman, the Congregational Church Missioner, performed the simple committal rites.

When Samuel Steel was brought before the court again it was commented that he had 'lost the spruce smart look' that had characterised him at his first appearance. He needed a shave and his confinement had marked him with a 'sallow countenance'. The known witnesses gave their testimony and Dr Lettis even offered to produce the fragments of skull he recovered from the murder scene. Removing a small brown paper package from his waistcoat, he was in the process of opening it when the Bench 'intimated that they would rather not see its contents'. Having heard the evidence, the magistrates formally charged Steel and committed him for trial at the next County Assizes. Asked if he had anything to say, Steel, speaking with apparent difficulty, said, 'All I have to say – is I know – nothing about the charge whatever.'

Samuel Steel was brought before Sir Henry Hawkins at the County Assizes held at the Shirehall in Norwich on 21 July 1898. A 'flutter' of excitement passed through the court when Steel was brought before the bar. Perhaps a little paler, instead of a bandage around his throat there was a scar visible just above his neat upright collar and tie. He still appeared to show little concern for his situation or for what was going on around him. When asked how he pleaded, he answered with a firm 'not guilty'.

The witnesses recalled the case and the medical evidence was presented but Steel was fortunate to have Ernest Wild as his defence counsel. It was known that through his life Samuel Steel had exhibited signs of epileptic mania, a condition that displayed vastly different behaviour in the sufferer than the more common epilepsy that was suffered by his father. Witnesses came forward to confirm these violent episodes; notably some of his old comrades from the 19th Hussars who recalled a number of outbursts, one of which when he frothed from the mouth and had to be strapped to a bed. It was clear from the testimony of the expert medical witnesses that the knowledge of mental illness and the various forms it could manifest were in their infancy. The defence counsel demonstrated that a number of expert medical witnesses had decided upon their opinion without awareness or consideration of epileptic mania and clearly established a history of the condition in Steel's family and personal history and emphasised this aspect of the case eloquently in his summing up. The jury were left to decide whether Steel had been aware of his actions and guilty of murder or whether he was guilty but insensible of his actions 'by reason of disease of the brain' at the time. The jury retired for over two hours and finally returned a verdict of 'guilty, but we wish to add that he was insane at the time'. The Clerk of the Assize asked for clarification: 'Insane, so as not to be responsible for his actions at the time that he did that act?' The foreman replied, 'Yes.' Steel was sentenced to be detained 'until Her Majesty's pleasure be known'.

DEAD IN THE WATER
GREAT YARMOUTH (1900)

———————❁———————

One fine day in late May 1900, William Rowe, a Yarmouth labourer, was working on the new bridge over Breydon Water, when his attention was drawn to an unusual bundle floating further up stream. The flow of the water was not so rapid that the object was washed away in seconds so Rowe went down to investigate with a log pole. It did not take much prodding and coaxing to get the object to the bank where it was soon apparent that it was the bloated and badly decomposed body of a woman who had clearly been in the water for some time. Securing the body, Rowe took it to Houghton's Yard where the riverboats were hauled up – the irony of this location will become apparent later in the story. The police were summoned and upon the arrival of PC Burgess the body was removed to the mortuary. A search of the corpse revealed a purse containing half a crown, a few pence and a small key. The body was soon identified as that of 43-year-old Mary Ann Carrier who had disappeared two weeks previously from her lodgings in Quay Mill Walk.

Mary Ann had been estranged from her husband Alfred, a carter who lived on North Market Row, for about nine months. He had told her to leave 'in consequence of her conduct with another man' and she had packed up and left. During the next few months the couple did not communicate. Alfred said he had found out Mary had taken up a number of lodgings in Yarmouth and Gorleston but had often had to move on because she had been found 'in the company of men'. He claimed he had last seen Mary in the Market Place on 10 May. Reading between the lines and in the light of her husband's claim that he had 'no idea how she maintained herself', the conclusion may be drawn that Mary had turned to occasional prostitution to supplement her income, although it was known she did occasionally work as a domestic, nursing a man who was ill in Gorleston.

Mary had lodged on a number of occasions with Sarah Ann Gillingwater on Quay Mill Walk and she was there on Saturday 13 May, the day she disappeared. Mary had been out drinking and had brought back a man named Sam Fisk (who later stated that he had been 'involved' with Mary for about two years). Sarah objected and having tolerated this once too often, she told Mary what she thought of such behaviour. Mary stormed out, only to return a few hours later to demand her things, including a half-sovereign she had given to Sarah for safe keeping. Sarah relented and said she could stay but Mary was having none of it. With all her possessions and money returned she stormed out again. Sarah never saw her friend alive again.

Fisk said he had waited outside and heard the exchanges between Mary and Sarah. He stated that when they were walking through Houghton's Yard, Mary threatened to throw herself in the river. When Fisk held onto her, she cried out, 'Let me go!' Fisk claimed he calmed Mary down and they then walked to North Quay where they said goodbye and he walked home. Hannah Harris backed Fisk's statement as far as hearing Mary shout 'let me go' and saw her being held by a man. Hannah shouted out that the woman ought to be quiet or she would call the police. The couple appeared to calm down and walked off. Nobody heard a splash or a scream. Nobody reported hearing another thing, and all that was found, in a boat in Houghton's Yard, was a hat, a handkerchief and a jacket belonging to Mary Ann Carrier.

The jury at the inquest returned a verdict of suicide but pointed out there was insufficient evidence to determine the deceased's state of mind at the time. The newspapers drew their own conclusions, calling it 'A Sad Story of a Wife's Shame' but we will never know the answer to the question, 'did she fall or was she pushed?'

DOUBLE TRAGEDY
FELTWELL (1908)

───────────── ❁ ─────────────

Feltwell is a sturdy village that nestles in the south-west corner of Norfolk, near the Suffolk border. In the early years of the 20th century, this area relied on agriculture for its main source of employment. Life was simple but work was hard for the population of 1,200 or so. Local folk still came together as a community to help with the harvest, worship in church or chapel and share celebrations and sorrows. In such a village, before the days of easy migration around the country, most families had lived there for generations and everybody knew everybody else, at least by sight. As the darker, colder months drew in and the winds began to blow across the fields and fens, nobody expected the horrors that were to be perpetrated in their close rural community.

Charles Wilson and his wife, Susan, lived a quiet existence in an isolated cottage just outside Feltwell. Wilson was a travelling salesman who made his living selling umbrellas around the country while his wife, a woman of 70 and some 17 years older than her husband, kept house. On 8 October 1908 Wilson set out on one of his sales trips. As he steered his pony and trap down the lane, his wife waved him off from their little cottage and he called back his promise that he would be back on Sunday. All seemed well in this rural idyll and after a reasonable number of sales he was glad to be returning home on Sunday afternoon. No doubt feeling his age and probably muttering, 'I'm too old for this game', he steered his pony and trap into the village. He looked up at the church clock, saw it was 3.30 pm and made a mental note he would be home by 4 pm.

At last Wilson reached his front door, just a few minutes after 4 pm. As he pressed his thumb on the latch it lifted but the door would not open. Charlie gave the door a good rattle and called out his wife's name – there was no response. Driven half by overtiredness and half by a growing concern for his wife, the man mustered up all his strength and forced an entry to his cottage. All thoughts of fatigue left him as he discovered the body of his wife lying on the floor. She had been battered to death with an axe. The terrified Charlie Wilson ran to summon the doctor and police.

As poor Mr Wilson was making his horrible discovery, another local man, 35-year-old James Nicholls, was stumbling into Maggee's Farm where he blurted out to two people there that Wilson had just murdered his wife. Seemingly shocked by the event Nicholls was taken to the local pub. Police investigations soon found two witnesses who shed some very clear light on the horrible events of that Sunday afternoon. After reporting the discovery of his wife's body to the authorities, it was to his friend Mr Southgate that Wilson went to await the arrival of the authorities. Southgate recalled he had seen Jem Nicholls, accompanied by his dog, walking through the village in the direction of Wilson's cottage at about 2.20 pm. Another witness soon came forward, a 14-year-old local lad named Banham. While playing in the fields near the Wilson residence he had seen a man, who he 'knew by sight and name' as Nicholls, enter the cottage. After about five minutes the boy's attention was drawn to the house when he heard screams for help from Mrs Wilson. Looking across the field the boy saw the old woman being dragged into the road, Nicholls momentarily let go of her, she stopped screaming, then Nicholls leapt at her and dragged her back inside the cottage. When Nicholls was seen to finally leave the cottage, Banham saw Wilson coming up the road in his cart.

The police lost no time in arresting Nicholls in the local pub and the whole terrible event rapidly became the talk of the county. The trial was held later the same month at the Norfolk Winter Assizes in Norwich Shirehall before Mr Justice Grantham. Much was made by the defence counsel of how Banham could be so sure of the identity of the man seen entering the cottage which was over 700 yards from where the lad had been standing. The boy was not intimidated and clearly stated that he knew Nicholls by sight and name and that he recognised him on that fateful afternoon by the clothes he typically wore and the dog with him. After demonstrating what time Mr Wilson returned home and how long it would take Nicholls to travel to Maggee's Farm, the prosecution pointed out that only Nicholls could have known about the murder of Mrs Wilson at the time he first reported it. Combined with the statements of Southgate and Banham the jury only took a quarter of an hour to find James Nicholls guilty of the murder of Susan Wilson. The judge placed the black cap on his head and passed the death sentence. Nicholls was executed at Norwich Prison on 2 December 1908.

A horrible postscript to this case was a second outrage perpetrated at Feltwell only two months after the murder of Mrs Wilson. On 14 December Ernest William Russell, a recently released convict, attacked Georgina Rowe in her shop with a blacksmith's hammer. Her piteous screams of 'Murder!' brought locals and the law running to her aid. Prompt medical attention saved her life but Russell had fled. The following day cries were heard by Mr Tibbett, a traction engine driver in the employ of Cock Brothers, who had gone to Tennis Hill Farm to remove threshing tackle. After investigation Russell was discovered hiding down an 85 ft well in 5 ft of water. Conveyed to Methwold lock-up he was soon brought to trial and sentenced to 5 years' penal servitude.

MYSTERY AIRSHIPS OVER THE COUNTY?
NORFOLK (1909)

---❁---

In May 1909 newspapers across Britain were full of accounts of unexplained airships seen and heard traversing the night sky from locations as far apart as Wales and Suffolk. To put this into context, the Wright brothers had only achieved powered flight in 1903; Bleriot would not fly across the Channel until 25 July 1909; and the first Channel crossings by airship were a year away. Anglo–German relations had been strained since the Germans had started building their own warships to rival the pride of the British fleet HMS *Dreadnought*. Furthermore, the distrust and perception of sinister anti-British machinations of the German people had featured in the popular press and literature for a number of years previously. In *Riddle of the Sands* (1903) Erskine Childers wove a tale of two young amateur sailors who battled the secret forces of mighty Germany. Their navigational skills proved as important as their powers of deduction in uncovering the plot that loomed over the international community. Other titles such as *The Invasion of 1910* (1906) and *Spies of the Kaiser* (1909), both by William le Queux, ably demonstrate the tenor of such literature.

In the spring of 1909 newspapers were reporting the successful distance trials of Zeppelins in Germany. In the climate of anti-German fears, many considered the purpose of these monstrous creations was a sinister one and wondered how long it would be before they came over England. East Anglians, particularly Norfolk residents, after centuries of watching the natural harbours along the coast during invasion scares, were particularly vigilant. Alleged spies and suspicious characters had already been reported at a number of locations. A year earlier, in 1908, the Secretary of State for War had been asked in the House if he could say anything concerning a 'ride through England organised by a foreign power' and whether he had 'received any official information or reports from chief constables in the Eastern Counties as to espionage in England by foreign nations'.

In March 1909 PC Kettle was walking his beat on Cromwell Road in Peterborough, Cambridgeshire. Upon hearing the 'steady buzz of a high powered engine' he looked up to see 'a bright light attached to a long oblong body outlined against the stars as it crossed the sky at high speed'. His report was met with interest from national newspapers but, no doubt fearing the panic such accounts could create, another police officer was sent to front the explanations. Kettle, it was claimed, had simply been mistaken. The whirring he had heard was attributed to the noise from the nearby co-operative bakery and the object in the sky was explained as a Chinese lantern attached to 'a very fine kite flying over the neighbourhood of Cobden'. The speed Kettle had said it was travelling at was just brushed off as 'a little poetic touch for the benefit of your interviewers'. However, more sightings of these mystery airships began to occur across the country.

The first published sighting in Norfolk was made by farm labourer Fred Harrison at Terrington Marsh, overlooking the Wash near King's Lynn. His sworn statement of what he believed he saw on the night of 21 April 1909 was published in the *Daily Express*: 'I was outside New Common Marsh Farm about a quarter to ten at night when I saw the airship. I heard a whirring noise overhead, and when I looked up I saw the fields round were lit up by a bright light. I was startled and wondered whatever it could be. Then I saw that the light came from a long, dark airship which was travelling swiftly overhead. It was low down – only a little way above the trees – so I could see it plainly. It seemed to be 80 or 100 feet long, and I could distinguish two men on a kind of hanging platform below. The searchlight lit up the road, the farm buildings, the trees and everything it touched, so that it was like day. I could even read the printing on some bills on the wall. The airship passed right over New Common Marsh Farm, and went in the direction of Hunstanton, on the other side of the Wash. It was travelling very fast against the wind, and it was out of sight in a few minutes.'

Other sightings were reported over the ensuing weeks from locations across East Anglia. Some thought the airship was the secret invention of a British aeronaut who housed his flying machine in some remote farm building between Market Harborough and Peterborough, but most were of the opinion the airship was German in origin and, whatever its mission, it was ominous. In one notable instance on Friday 7 May 'a long sausage-shaped dirigible balloon' was spotted over New Holland Gap, a mile and a half from Clacton in Essex. At a spot over which the airship had passed was found what was described as 'a stout ovoid dark-grey rubber bag, between 2 ft and 3 ft in length, enclosed in a network mesh, with a stout steel rod passing through the centre of it and projecting about 1 ft from each end. One end of the rod was capped with a steel disc resembling a miniature railway-waggon buffer'. It was thought that the object was some sort of fender designed to break the contact of a descending aerial machine with the earth. The bag was stamped 'Muller Fabrik Bremen'.

More concern was raised following reports of 'strange manoeuvres' in the North Sea by the German navy. Two large steamers were said to have entered the river Humber without British authority and then returned to Hamburg. The concern was that these ships had been performing some sort of reconnaissance mission. On 12 May 1909, Sir George Doughty, MP for Grimsby, raised the question in Parliament and asked if the manoeuvres had been 'carried out completely without being observed by any British guardship or other British authority?' Reginald McKenna, First Lord of the Admiralty, replied he had no information on the subject but would be glad if Sir George would communicate to him the details as they were known to him. In an interview with the press the same day Doughty said he 'did not have the slightest doubt' the manoeuvres had taken place at some time in the preceding three weeks and argued, 'The ports on the east coast of England are justified in urging that there should be some special protection provided for them', and concluded, 'No one can observe the action and policy of the German Empire during the last five years without coming to the conclusion that they have a definite object in view, and the natural presumption is that object is to strike a blow at Great Britain.' With the mysterious German navy manoeuvres in many minds, a notion grew that the mystery airships could have been launched from German battleships for their nocturnal sorties over Britain, a theory given greater weight when the *Shipping Gazette of Norway* published the story related by Captain Egenes of the Norwegian steamer *St Olaf*. He stated that on the night of 14 May, his vessel was in the eastern part of the North Sea when an airship sailing at low altitude approached and directed a searchlight upon the decks. After making a close examination of the *St Olaf*, the airship moved off and scrutinised another steamer in the same way. The gazette suggested 'the airship was carried by day in one of the German warships manoeuvring in the North Sea'.

On 14 May the *Daily Express*' Berlin correspondent had reported, 'It is admitted by German experts that the mysterious airship which has been seen hovering over the eastern coast of England may be a German airship. England possesses no such airship, and no French airship has hitherto sailed so far as the distance from Calais to Peterborough. On the other hand, the performance of several German airships, including the *Gross* airship, which has made one voyage of thirteen hours, would render it possible for them to reach the English coast. At the same time it is improbable that the German airship seen above England ascended from German soil. An aerial voyage to the English coast would still be a dangerous and formidable undertaking even for the newest airships.' However, by this date, sightings of mystery airships had been reported from Ely, St Neots, Wisbech, Peakirk, Orton and Wingland in Cambridgeshire; from Ipswich, Saxmundham, Bradfield St George and Woolpit in Suffolk and from Southend-on-Sea in Essex and even from Sandringham, where it was said the mystery airship had been spotted by the servants. The witnesses generally agreed the mystery airship was cigar-shaped, was at least 100 ft in length, the engines made a throbbing noise and it appeared to perform its manoeuvres with ease; some claimed to have seen the glare of its searchlight.

At about 1.20 am on Saturday 15 May, Mrs Fricker of Victoria Road, Great Yarmouth, was engaged in her duties as night nurse to Mrs H. Lawrence when she noticed 'a balloon-shaped object on the west side of the destructor on Caister Road. First it showed brilliant white, then a pale greenish light and next a reddish one'. She saw the airship sailing for about an hour and then tried to go about her business. When she looked again it was gone. The *Yarmouth Mercury* account of this sighting continues, 'Some perturbation was caused when it was seen the cock on the church steeple had disappeared, but it seems to have been removed by the steeplejack to be regilded, and has not been carried off to Germany by the aerial freebooter.'

Early on the morning of Sunday 16 May, Mr Edwards, a chief clerk for Lowestoft solicitor Seth Bailey, who had missed his last train home, reported that shortly after midnight about a quarter of a mile outside North Walsham 'something attracted my attention, and upon looking round and lifting my eyes over a fence I saw two or three lights, and they appeared to be a short distance from the ground. I paid very little heed to them and walked on. However, I had walked a few hundred yards when I again heard a peculiar noise, and this time upon looking round, I noticed a glaring light, and it seemed to be coming towards me. To make certain that there was something moving I got behind a large tree. I got into a position so that the light was entirely obliterated from my sight, and then I observed a dark object ascending. It passed over my head and proceeded in the direction of Yarmouth or Lowestoft.' Shortly afterwards, people in the Norfolk Broads reported seeing the lights of an airship. At 2 am on the same day, a number of people in Lowestoft reported 'a brilliant light' and 'a throbbing noise' as what they believed to be an airship moved in from the direction of the North Sea. Captain Hervey, Local Government Board Inspector for the Eastern District of Stuston near Diss, stated that at 7.45 am he was at Broome near Eye where he observed 'a cigar-shaped balloon sailing towards Lowestoft at a height of about a quarter of a mile and three or four miles distant. The airship was travelling in an easterly direction, a little south of Lowestoft and therefore going against the wind.'

On Monday 17 May the subject of the mystery airships was brought up in a debate in the House of Commons. Sir Arthur Fell, MP for Great Yarmouth, had asked Richard Burdon Haldane, the Secretary of State for War, if he could give the numbers of dirigibles constructed, or in the course of construction, by Germany. Mr Haldane replied that seven dirigible airships had been built, and another five were under construction, more than £100,000 being earmarked specifically for the craft in 1908. Mr Horatio Myer (Member for Lambeth North) followed up by asking Haldane, 'Will the honourable gentleman, in any report he may circulate, tell us about a certain dirigible supposed to be hovering about our coast?' This question was greeted with laughter, and no reply was received. On that night at between 8.30 pm and 9 pm, George Burwood, the skipper of the Lowestoft trawler *Red Rose,* was about six miles off Southwold when he saw 'a balloon high up in the air'. It carried no visible lights and was running before the wind in the direction of Ostend. It was even reported in the *Norfolk Chronicle* that our 'local

Coastguard are said to be in possession of "certain information" which may, or may not, throw some light on the matter.'

At dusk on Wednesday 19 May an airship at a great altitude over Shoeburyness was seen by a Royal Artillery Sergeant. At about 11.30 pm a well-known gentleman who resided at Wroxham was riding his motorbike homeward over the bridge when his lamp suddenly went out. Stopping the bike and dismounting to see what the problem was, the rider was suddenly hit by a powerful beam of light that appeared to be directed down upon him from the sky for half a minute. Dazzled by the light he could not see any airship nor hear any sound of engines but he was left in no doubt that it was an airship and in his opinion the ship was 'too high in the air for the whirring of the machinery to reach him'. Upon arrival home he told the story to his brother who said that while he was at Sprowston he had seen 'a strange light in the sky but could not see from whence it came'.

A short time later, a Mrs Turner of New Catton had her attention grabbed by 'a flash of light which made the street look like day' followed by a noise like 'the whirring of wheels'. She continued, 'I looked up and there I saw a big star of light in front and a big searchlight behind ... It was coming from the direction of the Angel Road School and flying very low, so low that it would have touched the pinnacle of the school had it passed directly over it.'

Mr E.B. Nye of Norwich told reporters that while others saw an airship at 11.30 that night, he and several others saw a bright light in the sky, which looked exactly like a falling star, adding, 'Had our brains been inoculated with the present airship scare, we might even have heard a whizzing noise, or had a searchlight directed upon us'.

A torpedo-shaped airship with a powerful searchlight was also observed by Mr Chathen, a young grocer's assistant, as he rode his bicycle through Tharston around midnight. Just after passing the residence of Mr Berney Ficklin he was also 'dazzled by a bright light shining right above him ... which brilliantly lit up the trees and hedges'. He noticed that there was a 'bluish tint about the light' which he said did not appear quite as powerful as a naval searchlight. It seemed to be switched on and off again in a few seconds. In a statement published in the *Norfolk Chronicle* Chathen said, 'I saw a long, cigar-shaped object, come three or four hundred feet above me. It was soaring upwards, the tapering end going foremost and moving rapidly in the direction of Norwich. On the underside was what I should call an iron bar, supporting a sort of framework, a yellow light shining at each end. I could not see any men upon the framework, nor could I hear any buzzing sound as a motor would cause but this is not to be wondered at because although the night was still, the thing was travelling at a great height. The sky was rather dark, but there was light enough for me to see the airship plainly outlined against it. I do not speak with any misgiving on the subject. I am confident about what I saw.'

The sightings of mystery airships over the county of Norfolk in 1909 ended as abruptly as they began. Most of the local and serious national press appeared to have tired of the stories and even spurned them. The *Yarmouth Mercury* commented that since the first 'flittings of a mysterious airship over the Eastern Counties at night time ... the halfpenny London press, hungry for sensation, have worked up a very fair scare'. Another batch of sightings occurred in 1912 across Britain, including Yorkshire, Kent, Wales and even over Hunstanton, and a flurry of sightings was made in 1913. Some strange and unexplained stories also surround the first ever Zeppelin bombing raid upon Great Britain over Norfolk on 19 January 1915, especially with regard to spies and the use of cars with powerful lights to lead the raiders to their targets.

Many questions raised by these mystery airship sightings still remain over 100 years later and those from 1909, before the Channel

Was it a Zeppelin 'scareship' that was seen in the night sky?

had been officially crossed by any flying machine, are by far the most enigmatic. No evidence has yet been uncovered in the German archives or from British intelligence to prove covert missions had been undertaken by Zeppelins over Britain under the cloak of darkness in 1909. So, what did the people see? It is clear far more people saw the airships and lights than those who gave their names and stories to the newspapers. Could all these witnesses really be mistaken or deluded? Perhaps Britain had been gripped by a mass panic or, tantalizingly, was there more to the mystery 'scareships' over Britain in those spring skies of 1909?

THE HYPNOTIC MR CLARKE
KING'S LYNN (1929)

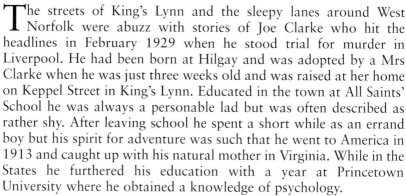

The streets of King's Lynn and the sleepy lanes around West Norfolk were abuzz with stories of Joe Clarke who hit the headlines in February 1929 when he stood trial for murder in Liverpool. He had been born at Hilgay and was adopted by a Mrs Clarke when he was just three weeks old and was raised at her home on Keppel Street in King's Lynn. Educated in the town at All Saints' School he was always a personable lad but was often described as rather shy. After leaving school he spent a short while as an errand boy but his spirit for adventure was such that he went to America in 1913 and caught up with his natural mother in Virginia. While in the States he furthered his education with a year at Princetown University where he obtained a knowledge of psychology.

Upon his return to Lynn, Joe Clarke was a changed young man, with confidence and a worldly-wise demeanour far beyond his 17 years. He confided in close friends that he intended never to have to work for a living because he had become a hypnotist. To tide himself over, he rented a room on Lynn High Street and set up business as a wireless dealer in the daytime, while in his spare time he cultivated relationships with dozens of young ladies, all of whom apparently succumbed to his hypnotic influence. His powers of conversation were described as 'out of the ordinary' – he seemed to know instinctively what would interest most young ladies. If a relationship appeared feasible, he would woo his prey with carefully phrased letters and beautifully composed poems that clearly showed Clarke 'as a man of poetic fancy and literary ability'. But what fascinated the ladies more than anything was his apparent 'gift of some mystic qualities'. All of them were quite unsuspecting that his diabolical plot was to hypnotise them and so exercise his power over them, not for sex, but so that they would happily part with their savings and keep him free from financial worries.

It later transpired his major source of income did not come from Lynn girls but from two others – one in Southampton and the other in Halifax, Nova Scotia. Both these women were blissfully unaware of each other or the deceit of their Lothario. Having met, been charmed and undoubtedly mesmerised by Clarke, these women wrote to him enquiring when they could meet again. Clarke replied in heart-rending letters saying how he was so ill he was on his sick bed, unable to work or pay for the medical attendance and comforts he needed to aid his recovery. Both women responded generously to the imploring letters of their 'sick lover'.

In 1926 Clarke quietly left several broken hearts behind him in Lynn and began an odyssey of deception and hypnotism across the country. He was eventually caught out and was brought up on charges of deception at Shepherds Bush and sentenced to six months' imprisonment. In October 1928, Clarke, now living under the alias of Reginald Kennedy, was in Liverpool where he encountered 19-year-old Mary Agnes Fountaine. 'Persuaded' to take lodgings with her and her mother at 110 Northbrook Street, Clarke soon began to weave his way into Mary's affections (no doubt to avoid paying the rent).

Mary's widowed mother, Alice, aged 47, was less easily persuaded and she took Clarke to task about his lack of a job. Perhaps he tried his best techniques on Mrs Fountaine, perhaps he was so shocked at his inability to mesmerise her, we shall probably never know, but Clarke lost all control and strangled her. He then strode into Mary's room and announced what he had just done and that he was going to kill her too. He attempted to throttle the girl but she fought back and, streaked with blood, managed to escape onto the street to raise the alarm. Clarke stood outside the house and enquired of the startled people standing nearby, 'Have you sent for a policeman?'

The police were soon on the scene and upon entering the house they discovered Mrs Fountaine's body in the sitting room, lying face downwards, her feet on a chair. After being cautioned, Clarke made a statement: 'I am 21 years of age, of no fixed occupation. I have been going to sea as a pantry-man. Since April I have been carrying on a little business as wireless engineer. An hour ago I had no more idea of murdering anyone than anyone else. I don't know what happened, but

Mrs Fountaine was talking to me about getting on and making good. She was saying that I should get a job and make a home for May. I can't tell what happened then but I suddenly put my hand round her throat and threw her over the arm of a chair. She murmured "Oh, Teddy Bear". That is the name she used to call me. I pressed her throat quite hard for about a minute, and she stopped breathing ... when Mrs Fountaine had finished gasping I went into the bedroom to Miss Fountaine. I asked her if she still loved me, and she replied, "You know I always did." I said to her, "I have killed your mother, and because you have turned me down I am going to kill you." I gripped her by the throat and she screamed and struggled fiercely. She disarranged all the furniture in the room but I eventually got her under control. Her lips turned black but all of a sudden she revived and struggled more fiercely than ever. I thought her screams would have attracted the whole street. There are some pieces of electric light cord upstairs, one of which I tied round her throat. She began to gasp like her mother had done. Then I suddenly realised I was killing her. I had in my pocket a shoemaker's knife, which is upstairs. I cut the cord round her throat and tried to bring her round. She screamed afresh. Then I cut her throat. She seemed to go quiet for a time. Then she recovered ...'

When he appeared at Liverpool Police Court, Joseph Reginald Victor Clarke was described as 'a man of slight build and clean-cut features'. When he appeared in court, he still bore a cut on his forehead from his fight with Mary. Clarke was finally brought before Liverpool Assizes on 4 February 1929. After the indictment had been read Clarke was called upon to plead and replied in a steady voice, 'I plead guilty.' Asked by the judge, Mr Justice Finlay, if he realised the implications of his plea and confession Clarke replied, 'Yes, my Lord.' Finlay asked again, 'You have thoroughly and clearly thought it over and understand?' Clarke replied confidently again, 'Yes, my Lord.' Finlay then replied, 'Very well.' The judge motioned to the Clerk of the Assize who asked if Clarke had anything to say. He said he had nothing to add. Justice Finlay then had no other recourse but to don the black cap and pass the sentence of death. From the moment Clarke had entered the dock to the final pronouncement, the entire trial had occupied less than five minutes. An appeal was lodged on Clarke's behalf but the conviction was considered sound and any grounds for intercession dismissed by Mr Justice Avory. Clarke went to the gallows at Liverpool prison and was executed by Tom Pierrepoint on Tuesday 12 March 1929.

DEATH OF A KNIGHT
HONINGHAM (1944)

----------❁----------

Sir Eric Teichman, GCMG, CIE, was a distinguished diplomat. Before his retirement in 1936, he was a renowned expert in Chinese affairs. He acted as Chinese Secretary in Peking and had been recalled in 1942 to become Chinese adviser to the British Embassy in Chungking. Respected for his long service and knowledge, Sir Eric was known affectionately by his many friends in the Foreign Office as 'Old Tai'.

In 1944, aged 60, he was back living in his Norfolk home, the magnificent Jacobean mansion that was Honingham Hall. Shortly after the outbreak of the Second World War, Sir Eric had offered the hall as an evacuation centre and a number of Dr Barnardo schoolboys were sent there. The ancient woodlands of the hall rang with the boys' shouts and so impressed was Sir Eric by the conduct of the boys that he invited them to stay. A contract was drawn up whereby Sir Eric acted as landlord, loaned a large part of his home to Dr Barnardo's while retaining the more stately area for himself and his family. He even changed his will leaving the whole of his estate to them, on the one condition that 'Lady Teichman would reside in her quarters during her lifetime'. This kindly and benevolent knight, however, was to meet a very tragic and undeserved end.

On Sunday 3 December 1944, at about 2 pm, Sir Eric and Lady Teichman were just finishing their lunch when shots were heard ringing out from the area of the woods on his estate. Perhaps one of the boys had acquired a pop gun? Despite the Normandy landings six months previously, there were still fears of German parachutists on one last-ditch mission, not to mention poachers – although it has to be said it was unlikely either of these would have operated in daylight. Either way, Sir Eric went out, unarmed, to investigate.

Honingham Hall (demolished 1967).

When Sir Eric did not return after about three hours, a search party was mustered but to no avail and at 9.30 pm it was called off. Lady Teichman was unable to rest and made another search accompanied by Nurse Childerhouse, the district nurse, and chauffeur Lionel Walter Cook. Shortly after midnight Nurse Childerhouse found Sir Eric's body in undergrowth about 500 yards from the hall. Death had evidently occurred some hours before. He had been shot through the head. The police were called and a murder enquiry was instigated under Detective Inspector Garner who had been despatched to the scene by Norfolk County Constabulary headquarters.

The inquest was conducted at Honingham Hall before the Norwich District Coroner, Mr W. Barnard, on 5 December. Significantly, a senior officer of the USAAF and Major Burch, United States Provost Officer were also present. Detective Inspector Garner described the wound caused by a bullet which had entered Sir Eric's right cheek and penetrated to below the left shoulder blade. He suggested that the blood tracks from the wound were well defined which indicated that he fell immediately after he was struck and did not move again. Garner added, 'The whole attitude of the body was that of a man who was shot as he was walking.' The Inspector then produced the bullet found in Sir Eric's clothing and described it as a .30 calibre carbine bullet similar to those used by the United States forces. He added that ten empty .30 cartridge cases were found, all within 50 yards of where the body was discovered. He also said, 'the ground was hilly and the undergrowth high and as Sir Eric walked in a bent attitude, his head would not have shown above the bracken.' The inquest was adjourned, at the request of the police, until 5 January 1945.

The type and calibre of the bullet that killed Sir Eric led the investigating officers to the nearby USAAF base at Attlebridge. The base was sealed and police began the process of questioning personnel. On 7 December, the American headquarters in Great Britain announced that the US Military Police, working closely with the Norfolk County Constabulary, had arrested two American soldiers in connection with the fatal shooting. A witness had identified two servicemen named Wojtacha and Smith leaving the base with their carbines on the day of the shooting. Both men were brought in for questioning. US Serviceman, Leonard J. Wojtacha of Detroit made a full statement. He claimed he and another American serviceman, George E. Smith Jr, aged 28, of Pittsburgh, had bought a gun licence and misguidedly believed it entitled the bearer to shoot anywhere. They had been firing at various targets, even a cow, when Sir Eric Teichman had approached from behind. He challenged the servicemen as to their business on his estate and asked their names. Smith made no reply, but spun round, levelled his gun and simply shot Sir Eric down. In the light of this statement Smith was charged with the murder and he made a full confession.

Smith was tried under American military law and the Court Martial, held on the base at Attlebridge, opened on 8 January 1945. The Court consisted of twelve members, including the Court President, Colonel Olin F. McInlay. Smith withdrew his statement, claiming it was obtained under duress and pleaded not guilty. Private Wojtacha testified that Smith had left to go hunting with a rifle: 'After passing Sir Eric Teichman's house, we both fired at a squirrel which jumped from tree to tree. I stood on one side of a tree and Smith on the other. Then Smith told me there was a man behind me. I saw the old man coming up. I started to walk towards Smith and glanced over my shoulder at the old man who was hunched over and was about 15 ft behind me. The man said, "Wait a minute. What are your names?" The next thing I knew a gun was fired.'

'Whose gun?' asked Major Brokus. 'Smith's gun,' replied Wojtacha who explained, 'After the shot was fired I glanced across and saw the old man lying on his arm. Smith said "Let's get out of here." We walked away hurriedly. Neither of us went over to the body of the man.'

The defence described Smith's actions as a 'purposeless, motiveless and idiotic act and submitted that a verdict of insanity be given. The whole act was so unlike anything a sane man would do, rather it indicated that Smith was a mentally disturbed character.' Medical opinions were presented from Major Thomas March, chief of the section of neuropsychiatry at a US service hospital, who had declared Smith legally sane and able to be tried but the man was, in his opinion, 'a constitutional psychopath, one who was unable to adjust himself to normal standards'. In a subsequent examination he had expressed the view that Smith was 'a borderline case of insanity'. Major L. Alexander, a neurology and psychiatry specialist attached to the US Army Hospital, said he did not think that Smith could be faking his condition; he agreed with March's diagnosis that Smith was afflicted by a 'constitutional psychopathic condition, emotional instability and an explosive, primitive, sadistic aggressiveness. His mental deficiency was borderline and his mental age was about nine years.' Dr John Vincent Morris, a specialist in mental diseases employed as medical officer of Norfolk County Mental Hospital, confirmed both previous doctors' views of Smith's mental instability. He had formed the opinion that 'Smith was an anti-social type, who deliberately refused to conform to army rules and orders'. When talking about the alleged shooting, he was asked if he realised that he might have killed Sir Eric Teichman. Smith had replied, 'I didn't figure it at all. I just lost my head. I didn't even aim at him. I fired a single shot.' Dr Morris expressed his opinion that Smith fired the shot irrespective of consequences, possibly because Sir Eric had interfered with his pleasure and he acted under an uncontrollable impulse.

The prosecution delivered by Major Brockus argued that Smith, by his actions, had forfeited his right to live and that 'by his calm, deliberate act of murder [Smith] had become a cancerous growth on the world's surface and must be removed'. On the fifth day of the trial, after hearing the closing statements for the prosecution and defence, the court retired for 45 minutes. When it returned the president read the verdict: 'The Court in close session and with secret ballot finds you guilty. Again in close session and with secret ballot the Court sentences you to be hanged.' The court did not accept the defence's plea of insanity and the verdict was unanimous. It was recorded that Smith left the courtroom handcuffed and with half a smile on his face. The finding and verdict of the court were immediately subject to review by the Commanding General of the appropriate US Air Division and subsequently by the Supreme Commander, General Eisenhower. Smith was advised he could make an application to President Roosevelt for a pardon.

Great efforts were made to have Smith's sentence commuted to life imprisonment; even Sir Eric's widow pleaded that Smith's life be spared. His best chance was a reprieve under the laws of insanity but despite a further assessment George E. Smith Jr went to the gallows at the prison where all Americans under sentence of death were held, Shepton Mallet in Somerset. The day of his execution was somewhat ironic, 8 May 1945, VE Day.

HEADLESS IN A NIGHTIE
COCKLEY CLEY (1974)

---- ❖ ----

According to the studies quoted on the Missing People website, the total number of missing person reports is likely to be between 210,000 to 230,000 in any one year; about half this number is made up of children and teenagers. People disappear for a multitude of reasons: they run away from relationships, perhaps abusive ones, or they just feel trapped, some simply can no longer cope with life or financial problems, some are suffering from mental illness. Many cases of missing people are resolved within 48 hours and most are cleared up within twelves months but some do take longer.

It is estimated though, that just 1 in 7,400 cases of missing people are the victims of homicide; of this minority, the majority are women aged between 19 and 29. These victims are sometimes never reported as missing because their disappearance is explained away by phrases such as 'She has gone back to her mother' or to coin another phrase, 'It was just one of those things'. No one suspects that this may not be the truth and that in fact there is a killer in their midst.

At about 7.15 am on 27 August 1974, 19-year-old farm worker Andrew Head was walking up the track to Brakehill Farm on Sir Peter Robert's estate. About 200 yards from the Cockley Cley road something caught his eye, some grisly remnant left behind by a fox scavenging in the undergrowth. But this was not part of an animal's carcass, it was a human foot. Investigating further, Mr Head looked among the dense bracken and willow herb where he discovered a figure wrapped in a brown plastic dust sheet. He recalled, 'I lifted one corner and that was enough – I could see what it was. I went home and phoned the police.' He had found the body of a woman dressed in a pink nightdress, her arms were bound at the back and her legs, bent at the knees, were bound to her body, she had been decapitated and the head was missing.

The police responded rapidly. Deputy head of Norfolk CID, Detective Superintendent Ivan Mead, took charge of the investigation. With him were Detective Chief Inspector John Riches, Head of Dereham CID, Superintendent R. Goodings of Dereham and Chief Inspector Douglas Warren of Swaffham. Home Office pathologist Dr Alfred Lintoft was called to examine the body *in situ*, after which it was removed to Ipswich for post-mortem examination. A fingertip search of the site was conducted and in the afternoon about 30 police officers with sticks and six police dogs searched the fields and hedgerows for any clues, especially the missing head and the murder weapon. Even the field of barley adjacent to the spot was harvested at the request of the police, with a detective riding by the driver to keep a close watch over the blades of the combine harvester.

At 7.30 pm the search was called off. An incident room was set up in the courthouse adjoining Swaffham police station and it was from that room at 10 pm, after receiving the post-mortem report, that DS Mead issued a statement: 'It is the body of a well-nourished female, aged between 20 and 30 years, height 5 ft to 5 ft 2 ins ... The body is in a state of decomposition.' It was thought she had been dead about two or three weeks. He concluded, 'The police are urgently requesting information regarding any woman of this age and description who is believed to be missing from her usual place of abode.'

The spot where the body was found was a remote one, a mile-long track running between the Swaffham to Cockley Cley road to the west and the A1065, Brandon road, to the east. It was surrounded by farmland, immediately opposite the RAF Marham rifle range, close to Forestry Commission land and on the opposite side of the road from Swaffham golf course. The nearest house, apart from Brake Hill Farm, was about a mile away. On 28 August, police activity around the site intensified as police officers cleared an area about the size of two tennis courts with powerful cutting machines around where the body was found and used pitchforks to search the wider area. More uniformed police with dogs combed the fields and hedgerows in the area up to the Southlands estate on the south side of Swaffham. A detachment from No. 5 regional crime squad was assigned to the investigation and 40 detectives began house-to-house enquiries in Cockley Cley. At that day's press conference DS Mead said, 'The fact she was scantily clad suggests she does not come from a long distance away,' but added, 'if someone was coming this way on holiday what better than to dump the body a long way from the scene of the crime?' He agreed the head might have been cut off to prevent identification of the body. Mead said the track that ran alongside where the body was found was one frequented by courting couples and he appealed to anyone who had been there over the past month to come forward if they had seen anything suspicious. He assured them he would preserve their anonymity.

The problem was that despite the spot being remote it was a busy one; people would picnic there, have nocturnal assignations; and, as a number of locals interviewed at the Twenty Churchwardens pub in Cockley Cley pointed out, anyone seen lugging a large plastic bag would not have drawn particular attention because many people used that area to dump their garden waste, especially grass cuttings. Strangers were not particularly noticed in the area either, the roads were often used by holidaymakers. Tourist attractions such as the model Iceni village drew many visitors in the season and if the pathology was correct the body would have been dumped around the time of the August Bank Holiday.

Despite the meticulous searches and enquiries, few real clues were forthcoming. On 29 August pictures of the nightdress in which the murdered woman was found were released to the press. It was made of pink nylon, was of standard length with a frilly halter neck and an inner lining lighter in colour than the outside, made to fit a bust size 34–36; it bore the St Michael trademark. There really was nothing special about the garment, available at Marks and Spencer around the country. There were around 10,000 of them already in circulation. The other item expected to be revealed by the police was withheld because, after further inquires, it turned out to be 'a promising lead'. However, the police were confident enough to announce that the woman had been killed elsewhere and taken to the spot, 'possibly in the boot of a car'.

On Saturday 31 August a mobile police station was sited at Swaffham's busy market to further publicise the police appeal for information. A poster outside headed 'Murder' asked 'Have you travelled along the Swaffham–Cockley Cley Road in the last month? Do you know any women who are missing? If so, the officers inside would like to speak to you'. DCI Riches later commented that after that day he was 'not too optimistic' about what they had heard.

Newspapers reported the police were anxious to trace the occupants of a dark-coloured British Leyland 1100 or 1300cc car that had been seen on the Swaffham–Downham Market road near the Beechamwell turn at 8 pm on Friday 9 August. Inside was said to be 'a man aged about 40, with dark hair, of slim build and wearing a dark coloured jacket'. The other occupant was 'a woman, younger than the man, with light hair rolled up at the back in the form of a roll or bun. She appeared to be asleep as her head was leaning against the door on the passenger side'. Police were also interested in a green Mini Clubman or saloon car which had been seen on several occasions over the previous month near the rifle range on the Cockley Cley road. The driver on each occasion was 'a woman of about 30 with shoulder length blonde hair'. This latter request got an almost immediate response and the car and driver were eliminated from the investigation.

Detectives continued their house-to-house enquiries over a wider area by visiting villages south of Cockley Cley such as Foulden, Gooderstone and Oxborough. On the following Monday, detectives flew over the site in a helicopter; by that time some 5,000 people had been interviewed, missing person enquiries were being made and followed up by other police forces across the country but still the investigating officers kept running up against brick walls; nobody was missing from the area and nobody had seen anything out of the ordinary, the clues simply petered out. What appeared to be promising leads were followed up but the missing women were alive and well (a number of them being none too pleased at being 'found' again).

The most promising lead at the time led to officers travelling to Great Yarmouth. That call prompted a late-night journey down to Surrey and interviews with a man and a woman. Detectives commented, 'We felt what they had to say was so important that they should come back to Norfolk and see us.' DS Mead met the couple at a campsite near Great Yarmouth and spent the day with them. What they had to say led to further inquiries being made in Torquay and Lancashire.

All came to nothing. The investigation carried on but no further developments were announced until 10 September 1974 when the last clue, the mysterious 'other item' earlier withheld by the police, was revealed at a press conference. It was the plastic sheet the body had been wrapped in. It was a National Cash Registers dust sheet used for covering data processing machines. Made from thin brown

NORFOLK CONSTABULARY

MURDER

ON 27th AUGUST, 1974 THE HEADLESS BODY OF A WOMAN
WAS FOUND NEAR SWAFFHAM, NORFOLK.   SHE WAS
AT LEAST 23 YEARS of AGE; ABOUT 5ft 1in. TALL AND
WELL BUILT.   SHE WAS WEARING ONLY THE PINK
NIGHTDRESS SHOWN ABOVE.   SO FAR, SHE HAS
NOT BEEN IDENTIFIED.

YOU MAY BE ABLE TO HELP
if

YOU KNOW OF ANY WOMAN OF THIS
DESCRIPTION WHO IS MISSING FROM HOME
OR HER PLACE OF WORK.

PLEASE CONTACT THE MURDER INCIDENT ROOM AT
SWAFFHAM 21825 OR YOUR NEAREST POLICE STATION.

The police poster appealing for help in identifying the victim.

plastic measuring 8 ft by 5 ft 6 ins, it was stitched and welded together and bore the logo NCR in screen-printed gold letters in the centre. Made in Dundee by a firm subcontracted to produce them, it was hoped this could have been a major clue. The problem was the subcontractors had closed down in 1968 and the folds in the sheet appeared to be those from the manufacturers, suggesting it had not been used much. The ever-hopeful police did ask if anyone had noticed such a cover missing from their place of work. Still the leads failed to emerge.

The last attempt to jog memories in the initial investigation came on 20 September 1974 when DCS Reg Lester, head of Norfolk CID, announced that all police forces in the country were being issued with an artist's impression that showed the nightdress the woman was wearing. He concluded, 'While we have saturated Norfolk we have to get a national interest in the hunt for this woman's identity.' Despite the nationwide coverage, enquiries with the FBI and Interpol, and an investigation during which 15,000 people were interviewed, 1,270 telephone calls were received, extensive house-to-house enquiries were carried out and almost 1,000 lines of enquiry were followed up, the investigation, while eliminating many possibilities was still unable to identify the body or the murderer.

On 24 December 1974 the inquest for the headless body was held at Fakenham. The post-mortem examination had revealed evidence that the body had been dragged along a hard surface and the head had been removed after death but the examination had produced no clear evidence of what the body had actually died from. Dereham District Coroner, Mr L.H. Allwood, had no option but to record an open verdict, the investigation was wound down in 1975 and the body was buried discreetly in Swaffham cemetery.

Over subsequent years occasional new leads have been offered including the possibility that an American serviceman from one of the USAF bases at Lakenheath or Mildenhall might have been involved but despite more investigations none of these came to anything.

In 2008 a cold case squad led by DI Andy Guy looked into the case again. Officers on the original investigation had been frustrated by their reliance on card indexes; it was hoped the technology and databases now available would reveal a new clue or someone's memory would be jogged by the revived high profile investigation. Permission was obtained from Greater Norfolk Coroner William Armstrong to exhume the woman's remains from Swaffham cemetery. The grave was reopened and at 4.30 am on 16 April the body was removed to the Norfolk and Norwich University Hospital for a second post-mortem examination, conducted by Home Office pathologist Dr Nat Carey. The body had been reduced to bones but these were mainly preserved well enough to obtain some evidence. Dr Corinne Duhig, a forensic anthropologist from Cambridge University, was called in. She found a 'slight change' in the pelvis that suggests, at some time in her life, the woman might have had a pregnancy – something that had not been detected in the 1974 post-mortem. A full DNA profile of the woman was also obtained and it was hoped it would provide a link to a living family member and a breakthrough in the case. The new investigation was reported across the media; it even featured on the BBC's *Crimewatch* with a reconstruction. New leads were offered but these missing women were traced as far away as Australia, New Zealand, Canada and Ireland; others were eliminated after DNA comparison.

At the re-interment of the body, Revd John Smith of Swaffham commented that it would be one of the saddest committals he had been asked to perform: 'I have done re-interments before, but we have known who the person is. In this particular case it is so sad that we don't know who it is – she is known only to God.' The search for the identity of the headless woman and her murderer continues.

BIBLIOGRAPHY

———————❖———————

Atholl, Justin, *Shadow of the Gallows* (London 1954)

Atholl, Justin, *The Reluctant Hangman* (London 1956)

Berry, James, *My Experiences as an Executioner* (London 1892)

Brend, William A., *A Handbook of Medical Jurisprudence and Toxicology* (London 1919)

Brookesmith, Peter (ed.), *The Alien World* (London 1984)

Butcher, Brian David, *'A Movable Rambling Police' An Official History of Policing in Norfolk* (Norwich 1989)

Childers, Erskine, *Riddle of the Sands* (London 1903)

Eddleston. John J., *The Encyclopaedia of Executions* (London 2002)

Evans, Stewart P., *Executioner: The Chronicles of James Berry Victorian Hangman* (Stroud 2004)

Fielding, Steve, *The Hangman's Record (vol. I 1868–1899)* (Beckenham 1994)

Griffiths, Major Arthur, *Mysteries of Police and Crime* (Special Edition) (London 1920)

Ketton-Cremer R.W., *Felbrigg: The Story of a House* (London 1962)

Mackie, Charles, *Norfolk Annals* (Norwich 1901)

Morson, Maurice, *A Force Remembered: The Illustrated History of the Norwich City Police 1836–1967* (Derby 2000)

Oliver, W., *An Inquiry into the State of Mind of WF Windham* (London 1862)

Queux, William le, *Spies of the Kaiser* (London 1909)

Queux, William le, *The Invasion of 1910* (London 1906)

Teignmouth Shore, W. (ed.), *Crime and Its Detection* (London 1932)

Teignmouth Shore, W. (ed.), *Trial of James Blomfield Rush* (Glasgow 1928)

Thurlow, David, *The Norfolk Nightmare* (London 1991)

Storey, Neil R., *A Grim Almanac of Norfolk* (Stroud 2003)

Storey, Neil R., *Norfolk Murders* (Stroud 2006)

The Missing People Website http://www.missingpeople.org.uk/

NEWSPAPERS AND JOURNALS

Daily Express
East Anglian Magazine
Eastern Counties Collectanea
Eastern Daily Press
Eastern Evening News
Family Tree Magazine
Famous Crimes
Illustrated London News
Illustrated Police News
Lynn News
News of the World
New York Tribune Sunday Magazine
Norfolk Chronicle
Norfolk Fair
Norfolk Journal & East Anglian Life
Norfolk News
Norfolk & Suffolk Notes & Queries
Norwich Mercury
Penny Illustrated Paper
Police Gazette
Reynolds News
The Criminologist
The Strand Magazine
The Tablet
The Times
Yarmouth Mercury

Other Norfolk titles published by Countryside Books

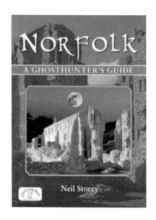

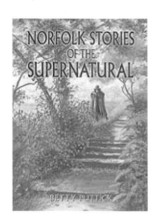

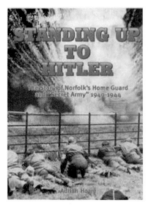

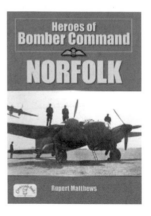